SAINT JOSEPH AND THE CARMELITE REFORM

OF SAINT TERESA OF ÁVILA

Studies in the Carmelite Tradition

SAINT JOSEPH AND THE CARMELITE REFORM OF SAINT TERESA OF ÁVILA

Father, Teacher of Prayer, Intercessor in Every Need

JOSEPH F. CHORPENNING, OSFS

Introduction by Steven Payne, OCD

*The Second Annual Lecture in Carmelite Studies at
The Catholic University of America*

The Catholic University of America Press
Washington, D.C.

Original text copyright © 2025
The Catholic University of America Press
All rights reserved
Copyright claim excludes images,
which are public domain or used with permission,
and the letter "St. Joseph, Patron of Carmel,"
which is reprinted with permission.

Cataloging-in-Publication Data available
from the Library of Congress
ISBN: 978-0-8132-3882-1 (paperback)
ISBN: 978-0-8132-3883-8 (ebook)

Contents

LIST OF FIGURES vii

INTRODUCTION *by Steven Payne* 1

SECOND ANNUAL CARMELITE LECTURE
   Saint Joseph and the Carmelite Reform of
   Saint Teresa of Ávila:
   Father, Teacher of Prayer, Intercessor in Every Need 5

ST. JOSEPH, PATRON OF CARMEL
   A Letter from the Prior General, O.Carm. and
   Superior General, OCD to the Carmelite Family
   on the occasion of the 150th anniversary of
   the proclamation of St. Joseph as Patron of
   the Universal Church 61

BIBLIOGRAPHY................................... 75

ABOUT THE AUTHORS........................... 83

INDEX 85

List of Figures

FIG. 1   Filippo Della Valle, *Saint Teresa of Ávila*, 1754. The Vatican, Saint Peter's Basilica 6

FIG. 2   Peeter Clouwet After Abraham van Diepenbeeck, *The Hermits of Mount Carmel Visited by the Holy Family*, engraving, 2nd half of 17th century, Spanish Netherlands. Private Collection 14

FIG. 3   School of Cuzco (Peru), *The Heavenly and Earthly Trinities*, c. 1690–1700. Philadelphia, The Frances M. Maguire Art Museum, Saint Joseph's University 15

FIG. 4   Workshop of Robert Campin, *The Mérode Altarpiece* (or *The Annunciation Triptych*), c. 1427–1432. New York, The Cloisters, Metropolitan Museum of Art 19

FIG. 5   *Joseph's Workshop*, right panel of *The Mérode Altarpiece*, c. 1427–1432. 20

FIG. 6   Joaquín Gutiérrez (Colombia), *Saint Joseph Protecting the Teresian Carmel*, 18th century. Usaquén (Colombia), Monastery of the Discalced Carmelites. 22

FIG. 7   School of Cuzco (Peru), *The Flight into Egypt*, 18th century. Philadelphia, The Frances M. Maguire Art Museum, Saint Joseph's University 25

FIG. 8 School of Mexico, *The Holy Family Enthroned in Heaven*, early 19th century. Private Collection 26

FIG. 9 *Saint Teresa Freed from a Three-Year Physical Paralysis by Saint Joseph*, engraving in Arnold van Westerhout, *Vita effigiata della serafica vergine S. Teresa di Gesù [...]* (Rome, 1716). 27

FIG. 10 Joaquín Gutiérrez (Colombia), *Saint Joseph Protecting the Teresian Carmel*, 18th century (detail) 29

FIG. 11 *Santa Teresa de Ávila*, pintura vidrio en Convento de Santa Teresa [*Saint Teresa Praying Before a Statue of Saint Joseph*, stained-glass window in the convent of St. Teresa]. 30

FIG. 12 School of Cuzco (Peru), *Saint Joseph Crowned and Enthroned with the Christ Child*, 18th century. Private Collection. 32

FIG. 13 Attributed to Marcos Zapata (School of Cuzco, Peru), *The Transverberation of Saint Teresa of Ávila with the Holy Family*, c. 1750. Private Collection 35

FIG. 14 Juan Bernabé Palomino, *New Teresian Foundations*, engraving in *Obras de la gloriosa Madre Santa Teresa de Jesús [...]* (Madrid, 1778) 39

FIG. 15 Niccolo Bambini, *San Giuseppe appare a Santa Teresa e la libera da un pericoloso incontro* [*Saint Joseph Miraculously Guiding Saint Teresa Through Mountainous Cliffs to a Smooth Road*], 1804. Venice, Church of Santa Maria degli Scalzi, Ruzzini Chapel. 41

FIG. 16 Francisco de Zurbarán, *La Virgen de las Cuevas* [*Our Lady of Mercy Sheltering the Carthusians*], c. 1655. Seville, Museo de Bellas Artes 42

List of Figures

FIG. 17 Miguel Cabrera (Mexico), *El Patrocinio de San José* [*The Patronage of Saint Joseph*], 18th century. Torreón, Coahuila (Mexico), Museo Arocena 43

FIG. 18 School of Mexico, *Saint Joseph Holding the Christ Child*, late 19th–early 20th century. Private Collection 44

FIG. 19 *Saint Joseph, Patron of the Universal Church*. London, Richmond upon Thames, Saint Elizabeth of Portugal Church 47

FIG. 20 Giuseppe Rollini, *Saint Joseph, Patron of the Universal Church*, 1893. Rome, Basilica of the Sacred Heart, Saint Joseph Altar 49

FIG. 21 "Solemnity of Saint Joseph, Patron of the Universal Church," from *Missale Romanum ex decreto Sacrosancti Concilii Tridentini [...]* (New York: Benziger Brothers, Inc., 1953), 560 54

FIG. 22 "Feast of Saint Joseph the Worker," supplement for the *Missale Romanum* (New York: Benziger Brothers, Inc., 1956) 56

INTRODUCTION

Guarding the front entrance of the Carmelite monastery where I live in Washington, DC, is a large stone sculpture of Saint Joseph of Nazareth. This follows a widespread custom among the Discalced Carmelites that goes back to Saint Teresa of Ávila herself. In *The Book of Her Life,* she credits "the glorious St. Joseph ... this father and lord of mine" with curing her paralysis during her early years in the convent, and famously recommends him as an intercessor in every need (*Life* 6.6–8).[1] Some chapters later, she reports that after communion one day she heard the Lord urging her to proceed with the founding

---

1   Quotations from Teresa's spiritual autobiography, *The Book of Her Life,* are taken from *The Collected Works of St. Teresa of Ávila,* trans. Kieran Kavanaugh, OCD, and Otilio Rodriguez, OCD, vol. 1 (ICS Publications, 1987). Numerical references are to the chapter and paragraph. Thus "*Life* 6.6–8" refers to the sixth to eighth paragraphs in chapter 6 of this edition.

of a new small community of Carmelite nuns more intensely dedicated to prayer for the church, where "He would be highly served," telling her that "it should be called St. Joseph and that this saint would keep watch over us at one door, and our Lady at the other, and that Christ would remain with us, and that it would be a star shining with great splendor" (*Life* 32.11).

In fact, Teresa entrusted her Reform to the protection of Saint Joseph, and when possible, dedicated each of her subsequent foundations to him, making sure they were supplied with his images. But in this respect, as the following pages clearly explain, she was simply building upon a deep love for the head of the Holy Family that already existed within the Carmelite tradition from medieval times. Today all the branches of the Carmelite family—laity, active religious, nuns, friars, and others of both the Ancient and Primitive Observances—look to Joseph as their patron and protector. And that devotion, as you will read below, has made a lasting impact on the entire people of God.

The Center for Carmelite Studies is established at The Catholic University of America through a generous endowment from the Carmelite Province of the Most Pure Heart of Mary. Our mission is to make the resources of the Carmelite heritage available to the contemporary church and world, by fostering scholarly study and research in the history, culture, and spirituality of the Carmelites, and by promoting the effective pastoral application of the results. From the beginning we have recognized that the riches of the Carmelite tradition are conveyed not only in the inherited texts of our great spiritual writers, but also through a myriad of cultural and religious expressions, including art, music, liturgy, devotions, and communal customs, as this volume shows.

When the Center first opened in 2019, we could not help but notice that, in the only stairwell leading to our offices,

Introduction 3

there stands a life-size statue of Saint Joseph, bearing the words "O custos Jesu esto custos noster" (*O guardian of Jesus be our guardian*) on its base. It seemed to suggest that this saint was watching over the Center's efforts as well. And when we began preparations for our second Annual Lecture in Carmelite Studies, we realized that it would fall within the "Year of Saint Joseph" (December 8, 2020 to December 8, 2021) that Pope Francis had announced to mark the 150th anniversary of Pope Pius IX's declaration of Saint Joseph as "Patron of the Universal Church." The occasion offered a providential opportunity to celebrate Carmel's abiding devotion to this saint and its importance for the whole church. And we could think of no one better qualified to address this topic than Fr. Joseph Chorpenning, OSFS, of Saint Joseph's University in Philadelphia. Working with Saint Joseph's University Press and others, he has been responsible for numerous studies on Saint Joseph and the Holy Family, many lavishly illustrated. Not only has he written and lectured extensively on Saint Joseph and the Carmelites, but he has been particularly sensitive to the way in which artists have explored and expressed this relationship. The pictures that accompany his lecture in this present volume offer a feast for the eyes and demonstrate the importance of imagery in handing on our shared Catholic and Carmelite heritage.

To the outstanding lecture by Fr. Chorpenning, we have also added another important document to which he refers, namely, a joint letter issued by the General Superiors of the Carmelites and Discalced Carmelites to mark the "Year of Saint Joseph." Not easily available elsewhere, it represents the most recent official reflection on Saint Joseph from the Carmelite family itself and provides further supplementary insights

Lastly, the Carmelite tradition—best known as a resource for deeper spirituality—has long seen Saint Joseph not only as a model and patron, but also as a teacher of prayer. When

Teresa recommends Saint Joseph to her readers, she adds that "especially persons of prayer should always be attached to him," and that "those who cannot find a master to teach them prayer should take this glorious saint for their master, and they will not go astray" (*Life* 6.8). Such advice might seem puzzling, since in fact none of the Scripture passages in which he appears explicitly present him as praying. But as Fr. Chorpenning and the Generals point out, Teresa's recommendation can be best understood in the light of her famous words: "For mental prayer in my opinion is nothing else than an intimate sharing between friends; it means taking time frequently to be alone with Him who we know loves us" (*Life* 8.5). Who better to teach this kind of prayer than the one who shared so many intimate moments with Jesus in the home of Nazareth? Our hope, then, is that words and images here may offer both greater knowledge and also spiritual nourishment to many for years to come. May the following pages inform the minds, enchant the eyes, and inflame the hearts of all who read them.

Steven Payne, OCD
Endowed Chair of Carmelite Studies
The Center for Carmelite Studies
The Catholic University of America

SECOND ANNUAL
CARMELITE LECTURE

*Saint Joseph and the Carmelite Reform
of Saint Teresa of Ávila*

FATHER, TEACHER OF PRAYER,

INTERCESSOR IN EVERY NEED

Since shortly after the canonization of Saint Teresa of Ávila (1515–82) in 1622, it has been a commonplace—particularly in devotional literature on Saint Joseph—that she played a decisive role in the development of his veneration (Figure 1). This role was described in a variety of ways: Teresa was "the first

---

I am deeply grateful to Father Steven Payne, OCD, and Brother Daryl Morresco, O.Carm., of the Center for Carmelite Studies at The Catholic University of America, for the invitation to present the

Figure 1. Filippo Della Valle, *Saint Teresa of Ávila*, 1754. The Vatican, Saint Peter's Basilica. Photo: Author.

to raise up the standard of devotion to Saint Joseph [...] by the care she took to make him known and loved by all"[1]; she was "chosen by God to persuade entire nations to devote themselves to this glorious saint"[2]; and "Saint Joseph would have been an unknown saint, had Saint Teresa not come on the scene and awakened this devotion."[3]

With the emergence of a more critical, scholarly approach to the topic of Saint Joseph, especially that carried out beginning in the mid-twentieth century at research centers

---

2021 Annual Lecture in Carmelite Studies for the Year of Saint Joseph. Catholic University is where I began to study Saint Teresa of Ávila: first, as a research project for Father (later Monsignor) Stephen Happel's course on the History and Method of Theology (appropriately enough, this lecture was delivered in the Happel Room), and then for my STL thesis directed by Father David N. Power, OMI. During those years and afterward, I also greatly benefited from the collegial encouragement and counsel of Father John Sullivan, OCD, in the field of Teresian Studies, as well as from the opportunity to do research in the incomparable Carmelitana Collection at Whitefriars Hall.

Unless otherwise indicated, translations are mine. All references to Teresa's writings are to chapter and section in *The Collected Works of St. Teresa of Ávila*, Vol. 1: *The Book of Her Life, Spiritual Testimonies, Soliloquies*; Vol. 2: *The Way of Perfection, Meditations on the Song of Songs, The Interior Castle*; Vol. 3: *The Book of Her Foundations, Minor Works*, trans. Kieran Kavanaugh, OCD, and Otilio Rodríguez, OCD (ICS Publications, 1976–1986).

[1] Paul de Barry, *La dévotion à saint Joseph*, 4th ed. (Liege, 1642), 82.

[2] Jean Jacquinot, *La gloire de saint Joseph* (Dijon, 1644), 344, quoted by Bernard Dompnier, "Thérèse d'Avila et la dévotion française à saint Joseph au XVIIe siècle," *Revue d'Histoire de l'Église de France* 90 (2004): 176 (hereafter Dompnier).

[3] Étienne Binet, *Le tableau des diverses faveurs faites à saint Joseph* (Paris, 1634), 458, quoted by Dompnier, 176–77.

in Valladolid and in Montreal, this commonplace was given a more precise formulation. For example, the 1974 article on Saint Joseph in the *Dictionnaire de spiritualité* puts it this way: "Teresa of Ávila plays an important role in the dissemination of devotion [to Saint Joseph] by both her example and her writings. [...] Her collaborators will spread this devotion at the same time as the reform."[4]

The Teresian commonplace is also found in the papal magisterium on Saint Joseph. In his apostolic exhortation commemorating the centenary of Pope Leo XIII's encyclical on Saint Joseph, *Quamquam Pluries* (August 15, 1889), Pope Saint John Paul II writes: "The Gospels speak exclusively of what Joseph 'did.' Still, they allow us to discover in his 'actions'—shrouded in silence as they are—an aura of *deep contemplation*. This explains [...] why St. Teresa of Jesus, the great reformer of the Carmelites, promoted the renewal of veneration of St. Joseph in Western Christianity."[5] More recently, in his apostolic letter for the 150th anniversary of Saint Joseph's proclamation by Blessed

---

4   Roland Gauthier, CSC, "[Saint Joseph] dans l'histoire de la spiritualité," *Dictionnaire de spiritualité*, vol. 8 (Beauchesne, 1974), 1311. Among Teresa's collaborators who disseminated her veneration of Saint Joseph were Blessed Anne of Saint Bartholomew (1550–1626), Blessed Anne of Jesus (1545–1621), and Jerome Gracián (1545–1614), whose *Josephina: Summary of the Excellencies of Saint Joseph* (first published in Italian and Spanish in 1597, with more than two dozen editions and translations thereafter) continued Teresa's apostolate of fostering veneration of Saint Joseph and of inculcating in the reformed Carmel a deep filial affection for this saint.

5   John Paul II, Apostolic Exhortation *Redemptoris Custos / Guardian of the Redeemer: On the Person and Mission of Saint Joseph in the Life of Christ and of the Church* (August 15, 1989), Vatican translation (United States Catholic Conference, 1989), no. 25 (hereafter *Guardian of the Redeemer*).

Pope Pius IX as Patron of the Universal Church (December 8, 1870), Pope Francis singles out Teresa from among the "[i]nnumerable holy men and women [who] were passionately devoted to [Saint Joseph]": she "chose him as her advocate and intercessor, had frequent recourse to him and received whatever graces she asked of him. Encouraged by her own experience, Teresa persuaded others to cultivate devotion to Joseph."[6]

In rhetoric, a commonplace is not merely a formula but encapsulates a theme to be unpacked and elaborated—very much like a plot is developed in storytelling.[7] In the present context, the theme to be unfolded is the story of Saint Joseph as a vital presence in Saint Teresa's life and Carmelite reform. Subsequently, this presence would radiate out from Carmel to have a significant liturgical-ecclesial impact, culminating in Saint Joseph's proclamation as Patron of the Universal Church. Equally important is the often-overlooked back story to Teresa's story, namely, the extraordinarily rich liturgical cult of Saint Joseph that flourished in the Ancient Order of Carmel. This was the fertile soil that nurtured and nourished Teresa's developing relationship with Saint Joseph, which fully flowered in the Teresian Carmel and beyond, to the universal Church.

---

6 Pope Francis, Apostolic Letter *Patris Corde / With a Father's Heart* (December 8, 2020), no. 1. All references to this apostolic letter are to the Vatican translation (by Helen Crombie): Pope Francis, *Patris Corde: Apostolic Letter on the 150th Anniversary of the Proclamation of Saint Joseph as Patron of the Universal Church* (Libreria Editrice Vaticana, 2021) (hereafter *Patris Corde*), with an appendix edited by Giuseppe Merola that includes the Decree of the Apostolic Penitentiary on special indulgences granted for the Year of Saint Joseph, the essay "Saint Joseph and the Popes," and Prayers to Saint Joseph.

7 Walter J. Ong, SJ, *The Presence of the Word: Some Prolegomena for Cultural and Religious History* (Yale University Press, 1967), 84.

I will approach this story in a distinctively Teresian way. Teresa is said to have "had an intense cognitive and affective relationship with religious imagery, as evidenced by the fact that she often describes her own visions as being 'just as in a picture.'"[8] She also "greatly prized and devoutly venerated"[9] religious paintings and images because they made Christ, Mary, and the saints tangible, present, and personal. For this reason, she took great care to place images of Saint Joseph and the Holy Family in each of the monasteries that she founded during her lifetime.[10]

Mindful of Teresa's privileging of the pictorial and the visual, the story of Saint Joseph, Saint Teresa, and Carmel might be envisioned as a "virtual triptych." A triptych consists of a picture in three panels or, in this case, a sequence of three different, though complementary, pictures, one on each panel.[11] These pictures depict three chapters in our story. In addition to facilitating storytelling, a triptych can also serve as a memory aid (*machina memorialis*).[12]

---

8   Carlos Eire, *The Life of Saint Teresa of Avila: A Biography*, Lives of Great Religious Books (Princeton University Press, 2019), 133 (hereafter Eire).

9   Kieran Kavanaugh, OCD, "Introduction," in *The Collected Works of Saint Teresa of Ávila*, 1:28 (hereafter Kavanaugh).

10 Christopher C. Wilson, "'Living Among Jesus, Mary, and Joseph': Images of St. Teresa of Ávila with the Holy Family in Spanish Colonial Art," in *The Holy Family in Art and Devotion*, ed. Joseph F. Chorpenning, OSFS (Saint Joseph's University Press, 1998), 24–36, esp. 29–30 (hereafter Wilson).

11 Figure 4, *The Mérode Altarpiece*, is an example of a triptych.

12 Mary Carruthers, *The Craft of Thought: Meditation, Rhetoric, and the Making of Images, 400–1200* (Cambridge University Press, 1998), 1–10, 22–24, 92–94.

Left Panel: Saint Joseph in the Carmelite Order of the Ancient Observance

To mark the 150th anniversary of the proclamation of Saint Joseph as Patron of the Universal Church, the Prior General of the Order of Carmelites of the Ancient Observance and the Superior General of the Order of Discalced Carmelites addressed to the Carmelite family a joint letter, entitled "Saint Joseph, Patron of Carmel." In this letter, included in this volume as an appendix, we find this synopsis of the origin and early history of veneration of Saint Joseph in Carmel:

> The veneration of St. Joseph is an integral part of our Christian formation, tradition, and culture. [...] [But] in reality, it was not always so. In the first millennium, the traces of a theological reflection on St. Joseph, or of any particular homage given to him, are very rare. It was only with the advent of the mendicant orders that devotion to St. Joseph began to develop. In addition to the work of the French theologian, Jean Gerson, a decisive contribution was given by the Franciscans and by the Carmelites.
>
> For Carmelites, interest in St. Joseph was a natural offshoot of its fundamental Marian orientation. Every member of the wider family of Mary [...] were the recipients of particular attention in Carmel. In that context, Joseph, Mary's spouse, could not be ignored. Pious medieval legends, in order to underline the close link with the family of Nazareth, Jesus, Mary and Joseph, [...] make references to visits that the Holy Family made to the sons of the prophets, the descendants of the prophet Elijah, living on Mount

Carmel. Others speak about a presumed visit that the Holy Family made on their return from Egypt. This connection must have looked so strong in the Church that some […] authors […] thought that perhaps the veneration of St. Joseph in the Latin Church may well have been brought by the Carmelite hermits on their return to Europe. This idea […] is no longer accepted […]. What is certain is that devotion to St. Joseph among Carmelites had liturgical overtones from the very beginning.[13]

Within the Carmelite Order, as recent scholarship has shown:

> the liturgical feast of [Saint Joseph] emerges in the second half of the 15th century, featuring an office which is entirely proper. This proper office is printed in the Breviary published in Brussels in 1480 and those following it, while the proper Mass is found in the missals published from 1500 onwards. The proper office […] was described as "the first monument erected in the Latin Church to the glory of St. Joseph" and undoubtedly constitutes eloquent testimony to the passion and fervour with which the Carmelites of the time honoured St. Joseph.[14]

---

[13] Míceál O'Neill and Saverio Cannistrà, "St. Joseph, Patron of Carmel," *Mount Carmel: A Review of the Spiritual Life* 69, no. 1 (January–March 2021): 2–3 (hereafter "St. Joseph, Patron of Carmel"). The citations given in the original source are omitted here, but reproduced in the full version of the letter in the appendix.

[14] Emanuele Boaga, O.Carm., *Celebrating the Saints of Carmel: A Commentary on the Carmelite Proper of the Mass and Liturgy of the Hours*, trans. Solomon Wright (Edizioni Carmelitane, 2010), 45 (hereafter Boaga).

The image on our triptych's left panel visualizes the Carmelite Order's historical relationship to Saint Joseph, and indeed to the Holy Family, from its beginnings in the Holy Land: *The Hermits of Mount Carmel Visited by the Holy Family* (Figure 2). This engraving, designed by Abraham van Diepenbeeck (1596–1675) and executed by Peeter Clouwet (1629–70), appears in at least two books that were published in the Spanish Netherlands (present-day Belgium) during the second half of the seventeenth century to memorialize the principal figures and events of Carmelite consecrated life.[15] In at least one of these volumes, this engraving is accompanied by a sonnet in French, whose first quatrain reads in English translation:

> Visible Trinity, beautiful stars, moving skies,
> Whose adorable countenance illuminates Carmel,
> O Joseph, O Mary, O Word made flesh,
> That you show yourselves readily disposed to favor us.[16]

These few lines of poetry help to explain the engraving's core meaning.

Of particular significance is the acclamation of Joseph, Mary, and Jesus as the "Visible Trinity," more often rendered as the "Earthly Trinity" (Figure 3). The term "Earthly Trinity" was coined in the late Middle Ages by Jean Gerson (1363–1429), Chancellor of the University of Paris, to speak about the

---

15 Fernando Moreno Cuadro, "Diseños de Abraham van Diepenbeeck para 'Les peintures sacrees du Temple du Carmel,'" *BSAA arte* 79 (2013): 157–81, esp. 167 (hereafter Moreno Cuadro 2013); and John B. Knipping, *Iconography of the Counter Reformation in the Netherlands: Heaven on Earth*, 2 vols. (B. de Graaf / A. W. Sijthoff, 1974), 1:156–57.

16 Moreno Cuadro 2013, 167.

Figure 2. Peeter Clouwet After Abraham van Diepenbeeck, *The Hermits of Mount Carmel Visited by the Holy Family*, engraving, 2nd half of 17th century, Spanish Netherlands. Private Collection.
Photo: Todd Rothstein (on behalf of the Author).

Figure 3. School of Cuzco (Peru), *The Heavenly and Earthly Trinities*, c. 1690–1700. Philadelphia, The Frances M. Maguire Art Museum, Saint Joseph's University. Photo: Author.

nuclear family of Jesus, Mary, and Joseph in the modern sense, because well into the seventeenth century the word "family" was generally understood to mean "extended family."[17] Within the Earthly Trinity of the Holy Family, Joseph takes the leading role in that he took the place on earth of God the Father for Jesus and Mary. This idea is rooted in Saint Ambrose's *Commentary on Luke*, in which Joseph the carpenter or earthly artisan (*faber*) is seen as a figure of *Deus faber*, God the Creator.[18] Joseph's leadership is also indicated by the order in which the members of the Holy Family are named in line 3 of the sonnet: "O Joseph, O Mary, O Word made flesh."

The pre-Tridentine Carmelite proper office and Mass for Saint Joseph present an equally robust theology and image of the saint. The readings for Matins are from Pierre d'Ailly's *The Twelve Honors of Saint Joseph*, which was condensed for use in the Carmelite Breviary.[19] Cardinal d'Ailly (1350–1420) was bishop of Cambrai and Gerson's mentor and predecessor as Chancellor of the Sorbonne. Gerson and d'Ailly belonged to an elite group of late medieval French theologians, centrally placed in the Church, who had thought deeply about Joseph

---

17 Irénée Noye, "Famille (Dévotion à la Sainte Famille)," *Dictionnaire de spiritualité*, vol. 5 (Beauchesne, 1964), 84–93, esp. 85.

18 Cynthia Hahn, "'Joseph Will Perfect, Mary Enlighten and Jesus Save Thee': The Holy Family as Marriage Model in the Mérode Triptych," *Art Bulletin* 68, no. 1 (1986): 54–66, esp. 58, 64 (hereafter Hahn). The "Mérode Triptych" mentioned in this article's title is the same as the *Mérode Altarpiece* described below.

19 See Bartolomé Mª. Xiberta, O.Carm., "Flores josefinas en la liturgia carmelitana antigua," *Estudios Josefinos* 17 (1963): 301–19, esp. 311–14 (hereafter "Flores josefinas"). For an English translation of these texts, see Cardinal d'Ailly, "The Twelve Honors Which God Bestowed on Saint Joseph," trans. Robert F. McNamara, *St. Joseph Lillies*, 34, no. 1 (1945): 22–25 (hereafter "Twelve Honors").

and conducted a campaign across Europe to rescue the saint from the neglect of earlier periods, to correct mistaken notions about him found in the apocryphal gospels and often reflected in art and literature, and to promote his cult.[20] The incorporation of d'Ailly's treatise in the proper office for Saint Joseph aligns the Carmelites with this effort by several of the most prominent theologians of the day.

The antiphons and prayers of the proper office and Mass exalt Saint Joseph as, among other things, the "father of the Church, with a mission superior to that of all other fathers," the "guardian of the Lord, providential husband of the childbearing Mary, and most pure guide of both," "our great intercessor in heaven," "the loving father [...] who nurtured the Sun of Justice in His cradle," and "the Christ-bearer [...] who brought up the Godchild from heaven."[21] Several word-pictures of

---

20 See Brian Patrick McGuire, *Jean Gerson and the Last Medieval Reformation* (Pennsylvania State University Press, 2005), 239, and McGuire, "When Jesus Did the Dishes: The Transformation of Late Medieval Spirituality," in *The Making of Christian Communities in Late Antiquity and the Middle Ages*, ed. Mark F. Williams (Anthem Press, 2005), 131–52, esp. 137–38; Joseph F. Chorpenning, OSFS, "St. Joseph as Guardian Angel, Artisan, and Contemplative: Christophorus Blancus's Engravings for the *Summary of the Excellencies of St. Joseph* (1597)," in *Joseph of Nazareth Through the Centuries*, ed. Joseph F. Chorpenning, OSFS (Saint Joseph's University Press, 2011), 103–36, esp. 103–6 (hereafter Chorpenning 2011). For an excellent overview and analysis of Gerson's landmark contributions to the theology of Saint Joseph, see McGuire, *Jean Gerson and the Last Medieval Reformation*, 235–39, 261–62, 295–99, and his essays: "When Jesus Did the Dishes," 131–52, and "Becoming a Father and a Husband: St. Joseph in Bernard of Clairvaux and Jean Gerson," in Chorpenning, *Joseph of Nazareth Through the Centuries*, 49–61, esp. 52–60.

21 "Flores josefinas," 314–16; and Tomás Álvarez, "San José," in *Diccionario de Santa Teresa*, ed. Tomás Álvarez, 3rd ed. (Grupo

the saint, presented by the proper liturgy, have parallels in the visual arts. To mention the most salient: According to d'Ailly, among the services carried out by Joseph for Mary and Jesus is that, through his marriage to Mary, "the virgin-birth [remained] concealed to the Devil."[22] This theme is reprised in the Post-Communion Prayer for the Feast of Saint Joseph in the Venetian Missal of 1500: "O God, who willed that Saint Joseph be united in marriage with the Virgin Mary, so that [...] he would be the guardian and foster-father of your Son, our Lord Jesus Christ, to deceive the devil [...]."[23]

In the *Mérode Altarpiece* (or *Annunciation Triptych*) of c. 1427–32 (Figure 4), one of the jewels of medieval art, Saint Joseph's workshop is depicted on the right panel or wing (Figure 5). There is a mousetrap on Joseph's work table and another on the windowsill. Their presence has been connected to a metaphor used several times by Saint Augustine in his sermons: "The cross of the Lord was the devil's mousetrap; the bait by which he was caught was the Lord's death."[24]

Editorial Fonte—Editorial Monte Carmelo, 2017), 663–69, esp. 664, 667 (hereafter Álvarez 2017).

22 "Flores josefinas," 311; and "Twelve Honors," 23.

23 "Flores josefinas," 315.

24 Meyer Schapiro, "*Muscipula Diaboli*: The Symbolism of the Mérode Altarpiece," *Art Bulletin* 27, no. 3 (1945): 182–87, esp. 182, and Schapiro, "A Note on the Mérode Altarpiece," *Art Bulletin* 41, no. 4 (1959): 327–28, esp. 327. Also see Hahn, 57. Johan Huizinga first discovered the symbolic meaning of the Mérode mousetraps in the *Sentences* of the twelfth-century theologian Peter Lombard (c. 1096–1160), as indicated in a note in the fourth edition of his *Autumntide of the Middle Ages* (1935). However, this book had already been translated into English in 1924, and so Huizinga's discovery largely went unnoticed, even by Schapiro. For his part, Schapiro found the original source in Augustine's sermons. See Johan Huizinga, *Autumntide of*

Figure 4. Workshop of Robert Campin, *The Mérode Altarpiece* (or *The Annunciation Triptych*), c. 1427–1432. New York, The Cloisters, Metropolitan Museum of Art. Photo: Wikimedia Commons, donated by the Metropolitan Museum of Art.

Figure 5. *Joseph's Workshop*, right panel of *The Mérode Altarpiece*, c. 1427–1432. Photo: Wikimedia Commons, donated by the Metropolitan Museum of Art.

Here, however, the mousetraps allude not to the cross, but to Joseph's marriage with Mary, which medieval theologians, such as d'Ailly, often spoke of as a ploy to fool the devil because it concealed the virgin-birth and Jesus's divine nature.[25]

This brief overview of the Carmelite proper liturgy for the Feast of Saint Joseph offers a glimpse of its theological richness and depth, which made a substantial contribution to the growing veneration of the saint that began to gain traction in the late Middle Ages. Saint Teresa was not starting with a blank slate in her relationship with Saint Joseph. She was "the heir of a rich tradition of veneration and devotion to St. Joseph in Carmel" and "would give more breadth and depth to [this] tradition, to the great benefit of Carmel and of the universal Church. […] [M]ore than any other, Teresa […] made devotion to Joseph one of the elements that characterizes the spiritual identity of Carmel."[26]

Right Panel:
Saint Joseph in Teresa's Life and Carmelite Reform

On our triptych's right panel is the eighteenth-century Spanish Colonial painting, *Saint Joseph Protecting the Teresian Carmel*, by the Colombian master Joaquín Gutiérrez (Figure 6).[27] This

---

the Middle Ages: A Study of the Forms of Life and Thought of the Fourteenth and Fifteenth Centuries in France and the Low Countries, trans. Diane Webb, ed. Graeme Small and Anton van der Lem (Leiden University Press, 2020), 508, chap. 21, note 1; and Bernhard Ridderbos, "Choices and Intentions in the Mérode Altarpiece," *Journal of Historians of Netherlandish Art* 14, no. 1 (2022): 1–43, esp. 18, and 42n90.

25 Schapiro, "*Muscipula Diaboli*," 185; and Hahn, 57.
26 "St. Joseph, Patron of Carmel," 5–6.
27 It is likely this painting is based on an engraving: see Fernando Moreno Cuadro, *Iconografía de Santa Teresa,* Vol. 3: *De las visiones*

Figure 6. Joaquín Gutiérrez (Colombia), *Saint Joseph Protecting the Teresian Carmel*, 18th century. Usaquén (Colombia), Monastery of the Discalced Carmelites.   Photo: Courtesy of Santiago Sebastián and family.

image serves to visualize the climax of the next chapter in the story of Saint Joseph, Saint Teresa, and Carmel, and shortly we will circle back to comment on it more fully.

Teresa may have possibly been exposed to some form of devotion to Saint Joseph in her home life. However, it was certainly part of her formation and liturgical prayer at the Monastery of the Incarnation in Ávila, where the rich Carmelite liturgical cult of Saint Joseph was firmly established well before her entrance in 1535.[28] For her part, Teresa would build on and greatly develop this solid foundation. This is the context for Teresa's statement, "I endeavored to celebrate his feast with all the solemnity possible" (*Life*, 6.7), which would take on a very specific meaning in Carmel:

> The custom of celebrating the Feast of Saint Joseph with great solemnity—with music and a sermon, bell-ringing, elegant flower arrangements and clouds of incense […]—[was] the custom in all the churches of the Order […]. Saint Teresa began it in the Incarnation and kept it up during the years she lived there. She continued it when she was re-elected Prioress, and used to celebrate it in the same way in whatever convent she happened to be staying on his feast day. This is one of the facts most testified to in the Process for her Beatification and Canonization.[29]

---

a la vida cotidiana (Grupo Editorial Fonte—Editorial Monte Carmelo, 2018), 44–46 (Fig. 20) (hereafter Moreno Cuadro 2018).

28 Álvarez 2017, 667.

29 Secretary General of the Discalced Carmelite Nuns, "Saint Joseph: Founder and Father of the Teresian Carmel," in *Saint Joseph and the Third Millennium: Traditional Themes and Contemporary Issues*, ed. Michael D. Griffin, OCD (Teresian Charism Press, 1999), 322 (hereafter "Founder and Father").

Teresa's devotion to Joseph, like that of the Ancient Order of Carmel, was liturgical from the start and had an essential liturgical dimension.

Entering further into how Teresa celebrated the Feast of Saint Joseph, she would have read and meditated upon the prayers and readings—Cardinal d'Ailly's *Twelve Honors of Saint Joseph*—in the Carmelite proper, which represented "the saint in all the splendor of his glory."[30] She was thus in direct contact with one of the principal early architects and promoters of veneration of Saint Joseph. Echoes of d'Ailly may even be heard in what Teresa herself wrote about the saint. For example, d'Ailly's fifth honor: "Joseph is honored [...] in being charged with the performance of many services not only for the Virgin Mother, but also for her Son."[31] Teresa: "I don't know how one can think about the Queen of Angels and about when she went through so much with the Infant Jesus without giving thanks to St. Joseph for the good assistance he then provided them both with" (*Life*, 6.8) (Figure 7). Teresa also takes d'Ailly's ideas to the next level. D'Ailly's twelfth honor: "Scripture tells us, not only the Mother of God and Queen of the Angels, but the very Son of God, was subject to [Saint Joseph]."[32] Teresa: "[T]he Lord wants us to understand that just as He was subject to St. Joseph on earth—for since bearing the title of father, being the Lord's tutor, Joseph could give the Child command—so in heaven God does whatever he commands" (*Life* 6.6) (Figure 8).

Saint Joseph's liturgical veneration at the monastery of the Incarnation grounded and prepared Teresa for a life-altering encounter with the saint (Figure 9). Not long after Teresa's

---

30 León de San Joaquín, *El culto de San José y la Orden del Carmen* (Juan Gili, 1905), 72.
31 "Twelve Honors," 23.
32 "Twelve Honors," 25.

religious profession in 1537, her health precipitously declined, and she became critically ill. Her doctors gave up hope of finding a cure, and in desperation her father took her to a folk healer (*curandera*) in a town at some distance from Ávila. The harsh, painful treatments Teresa endured only aggravated her condition. She returned to the Incarnation as an invalid who remained paralyzed for the next three years. Then, she regained her health as mysteriously as she had lost it—a cure which she credited to Saint Joseph: "Since I saw myself so crippled and still so young and how helpless the doctors of earth were, […] I took for my advocate and lord the glorious St. Joseph and earnestly recommended myself to him. […] For he being who he is brought it about that I could rise and walk and not be crippled" (*Life*, 6.5–6, 8).

Figure 7. School of Cuzco (Peru), *The Flight into Egypt*, 18th century. Philadelphia, The Frances M. Maguire Art Museum, Saint Joseph's University. Photo: Author.

Figure 8. School of Mexico, *The Holy Family Enthroned in Heaven*, early 19th century. Private Collection. Photo: Author.

From this moment, Saint Joseph had a preeminent place in Teresa's life. As already noted, the Carmelite liturgy employed a series of descriptive titles to convey Saint Joseph's mission and various roles in salvation history. Teresa uses a similar approach to explain the specific roles that the saint had in her personal salvation history and later in her Carmelite reform. A point to which Teresa returns again and again in her encomium of Saint Joseph in the *Book of Her Life*, chapter 6, is that what she writes about the saint is based on her own firsthand experience.

The picture that Teresa paints in her writings of her relationship with Saint Joseph is that its hallmarks were "constant presence, unceasing conversation, and great intimacy,"[33] together with firm confidence, warm affection, and a vibrant dynamism. What comes to mind here is Teresa's famous

---

33 Livinus Donohoe, OCD, *The Prayer of the Holy Family* (Carmelite Book Service, 2008, repr. 2009), 90 (hereafter Donohoe).

Figure 9. *Saint Teresa Freed from a Three-Year Physical Paralysis by Saint Joseph*, engraving in Arnold van Westerhout, *Vita effigiata della serafica vergine S. Teresa di Gesù [...]* (Rome, 1716).

Photo: Courtesy of the Carmelitana Collection, Whitefriars Hall, Washington, DC.

definition of prayer as "an intimate sharing between friends; it means taking time frequently to be alone with Him who we know loves us" (*Life* 8.5). This is the quality of Teresa's relationship with Saint Joseph, who drew and guided her into a deeper relationship and intimacy with Mary and Jesus, with whom he spent most of his life on a personal familiar basis as their provider and protector. Teresa's devotion to Joseph opened the way for her to share in "the experience enjoyed by Jesus and Mary within the warmth and intimacy of the Holy Family."[34]

Teresa experienced Saint Joseph in three primary roles. The first of these is as her father (Figure 10): "Not only was St. Joseph [...] Teresa's companion in her daily life, but she came to regard [him] as her father. In fact, she seems to have been the first saint to have adopted this relationship with him. [...] [L]ike Jesus, she learned to call Joseph her father. This was a source of confidence in her prayer to him."[35] Moreover, "Just as Jesus grew up experiencing the love and care of Joseph, who was His earthly father, so Teresa [...] saw Joseph as her father. [...] She trusted him as the one in charge of her life, knowing him, like the Child Jesus, as the provider of the household."[36] Apropos of this phenomenon, Fr. André Doze observes in his book, *Discovering Saint Joseph*, "God gave [Teresa] absolutely new insights on St. Joseph. [...] It is one thing to have had a glimpse of the eminent role played [in salvation history] by St. Joseph [...]; it is quite another to take him as a father with the full significance conveyed by this expression."[37]

---

34 Redemptus M. Valabek, O.Carm., *Mary, Mother of Carmel: Our Lady and the Saints of Carmel*, Vol. 1 (Edizioni Carmelitane, 2001), 101 (hereafter Valabek).

35 Donohoe, 88.

36 Donohoe, 90.

37 André Doze, *Discovering Saint Joseph*, trans. Florestine Audett, RJM (St Pauls, 1991), 34 (hereafter Doze).

Figure 10. Joaquín Gutiérrez (Colombia), *Saint Joseph Protecting the Teresian Carmel*, 18th century (detail). See Figure 6 credit.

Teresa's adoption of Saint Joseph as her father was unprecedented and thus groundbreaking. So too was her discovery of the saint as a teacher of prayer, which she succinctly expounds in three sentences in her *Life*, chapter 6 (Figure 11). By identifying Joseph as the saint to whom "persons of prayer should always be attached" (*Life* 6.8), as well as a guide for those "who cannot find a master to teach them prayer" (*Life* 6.8), Teresa establishes a firm link between the saint and the contemplative life of prayer. Undergirding this bond is Joseph's unique relationship of intimacy with Jesus and Mary. According to the Discalced Carmelite friar Jerónimo Gracián, who was Teresa's closest collaborator in her reform and in disseminating devotion to Saint Joseph, "St. Joseph learned prayer from the two most excellent teachers that can ever be imagined: Jesus and Mary. He prayed in their company, and these same two persons, whom he

Figure 11. *Santa Teresa de Ávila*, pintura vidrio en Convento de Santa Teresa [*Saint Teresa Praying Before a Statue of Saint Joseph*, stained-glass window in the convent of St. Teresa]. Photo: Wikimedia Commons, Xauxa, 2004.

commanded as subjects, he prayed to as God and as the Mother of God. No one else has ever had this privilege of prayer."[38] In this connection, Teresa's understanding of mental prayer bears repeating: it is "nothing else than an intimate sharing between friends; it means taking time frequently to be alone with Him who we know loves us" (*Life* 8.5).

---

38   Jerónimo Gracián, *Just Man, Husband of Mary, Guardian of Christ: An Anthology of Readings from Jerónimo Gracián's "Summary of the Excellencies of St. Joseph" (1597)*, trans. and ed. (with an introductory essay and commentary) Joseph F. Chorpenning, OSFS, 2nd ed. (Saint Joseph's University Press, 1995), 261 (hereafter *Just Man*).

With this understanding of what prayer is for St. Teresa, we can see why she proposes St. Joseph as the greatest master in this domain. St. Joseph's life, his vocation and mission were totally spent in Jesus's company and at His side as he spoke with Him and served Him. [...] Joseph's life found its meaning centered on Jesus: receiving Him and placing Him in His mother's arms, giving Him His name, guarding and watching over Him, feeding and teaching Him, living in intimacy [...] with Jesus. [...]

Indeed, Joseph's whole life was a prayer, because it was spent in Jesus's intimate company. No one was more familiar with this kind of prayer than St. Joseph, who spent so much of his time with Jesus and Mary in an authentic communion of friendship and love.[39]

Teresa's characterization of Saint Joseph as an unfailing heavenly intercessor in every need is not original to her (Figure 12). This idea was first put forth by Teresa's late medieval predecessors, for example, Gerson and the Italian Franciscan preacher Saint Bernardine of Siena (1380–1444).[40] It was reiterated by the Observant Franciscan friar Bernardino de Laredo (1492–c. 1540) in the short treatise on Saint Joseph he appended to his *Ascent of Mount Sion* (first edition, 1535; second edition, 1538), which was one of the books on the spiritual life that Teresa found most helpful in trying to explain her own experience (*Life* 23.12).[41] However, Teresa

---

39 "Founder and Father," 324–25.
40 Chorpenning 2011, 105.
41 See Joseph F. Chorpenning, "Bernardino de Laredo's *Treatise on the Mysteries of St. Joseph* and the Evangelization of Mexico," in *The Mystical Gesture: Essays on Medieval and Early Modern Spiritual*

Figure 12. School of Cuzco (Peru), *Saint Joseph Crowned and Enthroned with the Christ Child*, 18th century. Private Collection. Photo: Author.

develops this theme with such clarity, force, and certitude that it gained singular authority, coming to be universally regarded as a characteristically Teresian teaching on Saint Joseph.[42] This is how Teresa articulates this theme:

Culture in Honor of Mary E. Giles, ed. Robert Boenig (Ashgate, 2000), 67–77, esp. 75–76.

42 Dompnier, 181.

> I don't recall [...] ever having petitioned [Saint Joseph] for anything that he failed to grant. It is an amazing thing the great many favors God has granted me through the mediation of this blessed saint, the dangers I was freed from both of body and soul. For with other saints it seems the Lord has given them grace to be of help in one need, whereas with this glorious saint I have experience that he helps in all our needs and that the Lord wants us to understand that just as He was subject to St. Joseph on earth [...] so in heaven God does whatever he commands (*Life*, 6.6).

There is also a dynamic dimension to Teresa's interaction with Saint Joseph as intercessor: "[F]or some years now I have asked him for something on his feast day, and my petition is always granted. If the request is somewhat out of line, he rectifies it for my greater good" (*Life*, 6.8). Teresa describes her "experience of the goods this glorious saint obtains from God" as "impressive" (*Life*, 6.8)—an assertion which is corroborated by the care she takes to document these favors throughout her writings.

Through her prayerful intimacy with and confidence in Saint Joseph, Teresa was guided into a comparably deep relationship with the Holy Family and, also, to discover her mission in Carmel. Teresa is one of those rare individuals in Christian history who has a profound consciousness of the inseparability and integrity of Jesus, Mary, and Joseph. She encountered them "as living human beings, with whom one could speak on familiar terms, who answered you, who were interested in you."[43] In the artistic tradition, Teresa's intimacy with the Holy Family was visually memorialized by depicting Jesus, Mary, and Joseph as the primary actors in her most

---

43 Doze, 53.

famous and frequently represented mystical experience, known as the transverberation, a word derived from the Latin *transverberare*, meaning "to pierce through." According to Teresa, around 1560 she had a vision of an angel plunging a large gold arrow, with fire at its tip, into her heart several times, causing intense pain, but leaving her "all on fire with great love of God" (*Life*, 29.13). In images that circulated both in Europe and in the New World, engravers and painters significantly reinterpreted Teresa's account of the transverberation by substituting the Holy Family for the angel: the Christ Child shoots arrows at Teresa, while Mary holds the next arrow to be shot and Joseph helps Jesus to aim His bow (Figure 13).[44]

As she progressed in the spiritual life and experienced an intense period of mystical graces, Teresa discerned that she was being called to found a new kind of Carmelite monastery. Teresa "saw the Carmelite ideal as something good in itself, without the need of beginning a new Order."[45] The basic goal of Teresa's reform was a retrieval of the primitive Carmelite charism, with a view to living it more deeply.

During Teresa's days at the Incarnation, about 200 persons, including servants and nuns' relatives, lived there. However, the Incarnation was, as one scholar has recently put it, "no haven for slackers."[46]

> Contrary to common belief, religious life at the Incarnation was austere. Days each week were set

---

[44] On the transverberation as a subject in Teresian art, see Wilson, 24–25, and Wilson, "Saint Teresa of Ávila's Martyrdom: Images of Her Transverberation in Mexican Colonial Painting," *Anales del Instituto de Investigaciones Estéticas* 74–75 (1999): 211–33; and Moreno Cuadro 2018, 135–299.

[45] Valabek, 107.

[46] Eire, 11.

Figure 13. Attributed to Marcos Zapata (School of Cuzco, Peru), *The Transverberation of Saint Teresa of Ávila with the Holy Family*, c. 1750. Private Collection.   Photo: Courtesy of Saint Joseph's University Press.

aside for fasting and abstinence; silence was carefully maintained so as to encourage the spirit of continual prayer. With many kinds of detailed, minute rubrics, the Divine Office was celebrated in solemnity and splendor. No time, however, was designated in the legislation for mental prayer—a deficiency not without its drawbacks in what must have been a crowded monastery.[47]

Teresa envisioned something very different from what she experienced at the Incarnation: a strictly enclosed small community of twelve nuns and a prioress—this number modeled on Jesus and the Apostles—who would observe, like the first Carmelite desert hermits, absolute poverty, a commitment to silent prayer, and eremitical solitude, while devoting themselves to an apostolate of prayer to assist the Church in rescuing souls being lost in Europe by the spread of Protestantism and in the New World through ignorance of the Gospel (see *Way of Perfection*, chapter 1, and *Book of the Foundations*, 1.7–8). Thus, Teresa sought to retrieve Carmel's original eremitical charism, while contemporizing it by giving it an apostolic and ecclesial dimension. This was one of Teresa's most original and innovative insights: the contemplative life was not an end in itself, which was the traditional view, but had an intrinsic apostolic dimension, which brings it into communion with the whole Church.[48]

---

47 Kavanaugh, 19.

48 Tomás Álvarez, OCD, *St. Teresa of Avila: 100 Themes on Her Life and Work*, trans. Kieran Kavanaugh, OCD (ICS Publications, 2011), 135–38 (The Charism of the Teresian Carmel); and Salvador Ros García, "El carisma del Carmelo vivido e interpretado por santa Teresa," in *La recepción de los místicos Teresa de Jesús y Juan de la Cruz: Ávila, 20–26 de septiembre de 1996*,

This became a reality with the foundation of Saint Joseph's in Ávila on August 24, 1562. Prior to its foundation, Teresa had a vision in which God revealed what He wished the world of the Teresian Carmel to be: the "little dwelling corner" and "abode" of the Holy Family (*Life*, 35.12):

> One day after Communion, His Majesty earnestly commanded me to strive for this new monastery with all my powers, and He made great promises that it would be founded and that He would be highly served in it. He said it should be called St. Joseph and that this saint would keep watch over us at one door, and our Lady at the other, that Christ would remain with us, and that it would be a star shining with great splendor (*Life* 32.11).

The Holy Family of Jesus, Mary, and Joseph is, therefore, "meant to be the milieu in which the Carmelite is immersed."[49]

Teresa's intensely personal relationship with Saint Joseph and the Holy Family thus became the inspiration, model, and paradigm for the reformed Carmel. Saint Joseph as Teresa's father, teacher of prayer, and intercessor in every need now fulfilled these same roles for the Teresian Carmel as well.[50] Before her death in 1582, Teresa founded sixteen

---

ed. Salvador Ros García (Ediciones Universidad Pontificia, 1997), 537–72, esp. 566.

49 Valabek, 104.

50 Like Teresa's insistence on Saint Joseph being an unfailing heavenly intercessor, her understanding of the saint as teacher of prayer spread far beyond Carmel. More specifically, the latter took center stage in the crisis of mysticism which unfolded in the Society of Jesus. Beginning in the last quarter of the sixteenth century, the Jesuit order took an "anti-mystic turn," losing touch with its

more reformed Carmelite monasteries on the model of Saint Joseph's in Ávila (*Foundations*, 3.18, 9.1). Altogether, twelve of Teresa's foundations were named for Saint Joseph. Each of these likewise became the dwelling place of the Holy Family.

Saint Joseph accompanied Teresa at every step of the way as she worked to accomplish her mission of reforming Carmel. He had an active hand in the founding of both Saint Joseph's in Ávila and Teresa's subsequent foundations. Teresa placed a statue of the saint above the principal door of all the monasteries she founded, carrying "with her to [these] foundations a statue of this glorious saint" and "calling him the founder of this Order" (Figure 14).[51] Saint Joseph helped Teresa to overcome

---

> own mystical origins—epitomized by the well-known vision of St. Ignatius of Loyola (1491–1556) in the chapel of La Storta—and redefining itself by giving priority to its institutional and pastoral aspects over contemplative prayer, which had been championed by Ignatius. One form this anti-mystic turn took was Father General Everard Mercurian (1514–1580) urging Jesuits to disassociate themselves from contemplative groups and orders, such as the Teresian Carmel. Another was a letter of April 5, 1629, to the Provincial Superior of Paris from Father General Muzio Viteleschi (1563–1645), who forbade young Jesuits in formation to continue venerating Saint Joseph in a "new and unusual manner," alluding to their embrace of the Teresian advocation of the saint as teacher of prayer and patron of the contemplative life. For fuller treatment of this fascinating chapter in Jesuit history, see Rob Faesen, SJ, "The Grand Silence of St. Joseph: Devotion to St. Joseph and the Seventeenth-Century Crisis of Mysticism in the Jesuit Order," in Chorpenning, *Joseph of Nazareth Through the Centuries*, 137–50; and Facundo Sebastián Macías, "Hagiography as a Platform for Internal Catholic Debate in Early Modern Europe: Francisco de Ribera's *La vida de la Madre Teresa de Jesus* (1590) and the Defense of a Contemplative Way Inside the Jesuit Order," *Church History* 89, no. 2 (2020): 288–306.

51 *Just Man*, 242.

Figure 14. Juan Bernabé Palomino, *New Teresian Foundations*, engraving in *Obras de la gloriosa Madre Santa Teresa de Jesús [...]* (Madrid, 1778). Photo: Todd Rothstein (on behalf of the Author).

what seemed to be insurmountable obstacles in making her foundations. When Teresa lacked funds to pay workmen, Saint Joseph provided them. Gracián, who worked hand in hand with Teresa as she carried out her reform, attests: "In addition to the manner in which the glorious St. Joseph miraculously intervened in the building of this monastery [= Saint Joseph's in Ávila], he intervened in the construction of many others, both of the friars and of the nuns, so much so that it seems that it would have been impossible for these monasteries to have been built if this glorious saint had not taken them under his protection."[52] Saint Joseph also protected Teresa and her nuns on their perilous journeys throughout Spain to make new foundations, with the most well-known example being when he miraculously guided them through dangerous mountainous cliffs onto a smooth road while traveling to found the monastery of Beas in 1574 (Figure 15).[53]

This brings us back to the right wing of our virtual triptych. Gutiérrez's painting is emblematic of where consideration of Saint Joseph's vital presence in Teresa's life and Carmelite reform leads. The protection provided by Saint Joseph to the Teresian Carmel is symbolized by his cloak, which he extends to envelop one of Teresa's monasteries, giving flight to demons pursued by an angel. Images of the Virgin Mary sheltering under her cloak the members of a religious order, or other devotees seeking her protection, date to the middle of the thirteenth century (Figure 16).[54] By the eighteenth century, this was also a popular motif in Saint Joseph's iconography.[55] Besides interpretations of this

---

52 *Just Man*, 243.

53 *Just Man*, 245–46.

54 Michael Morris, OP, *Regina Coeli: Art and Essays on the Blessed Virgin Mary* (Magnificat, 2016), 134.

55 See, e.g., Teresa Gisbert de Mesa, "Gaspar Miguel de Berrío (Bolivian, 1706–c. 1762), *The Patronage of Saint Joseph*," in *The*

Figure 15. Niccolo Bambini, *San Giuseppe appare a Santa Teresa e la libera da un pericoloso incontro [Saint Joseph Miraculously Guiding Saint Teresa Through Mountainous Cliffs to a Smooth Road]*, 1804. Venice, Church of Santa Maria degli Scalzi, Ruzzini Chapel.   Photo: Wikimedia Commons, Didier Descouens. May 31, 2016.

theme on a grand theatrical scale (Figure 17), more intimate images intended for private devotion also adopt this motif, with Saint Joseph tenderly holding Jesus, while protectively enfolding Him within his cloak (Figure 18).[56]

Arts in Latin America 1492–1820, organized by Joseph J. Rishel with Suzanne Stratton-Pruitt (Philadelphia Museum of Art / Yale University Press, 2006), 443.

56   Joseph F. Chorpenning, OSFS, "Icon of Family and Religious

Figure 16. Francisco de Zurbarán, *La Virgen de las Cuevas* [*Our Lady of Mercy Sheltering the Carthusians*], c. 1655. Seville, Museo de Bellas Artes.   Photo: Wikimedia Commons, Paul Hermans, March 22, 2011.

In Guitérrez's painting, Joseph's paternal gaze is fixed on Teresa. For her part, Teresa gestures so as to draw the viewer's attention to Joseph, but she is not looking at him. Rather, she looks off, perhaps suggesting this scene is an interior vision in the mind's eye, which the viewer or votary has the privilege of seeing.

Life: The Historical Development of the Holy Family Devotion," in *The Holy Family as Prototype of the Civilization of Love: Images from the Viceregal Americas*, ed. Joseph F. Chorpenning, OSFS (Saint Joseph's University Press, 1996), 3–39, esp. 20.

Figure 17. Miguel Cabrera (Mexico), *El Patrocinio de San José* [*The Patronage of Saint Joseph*], 18th century. Torreón, Coahuila (Mexico), Museo Arocena. Photo: Wikimedia Commons, photographer unknown.

Figure 18. School of Mexico, *Saint Joseph Holding the Christ Child*, late 19th–early 20th century. Private Collection.   Photo: Author.

Center Panel:
Saint Joseph as Patron of the Universal Church

The final chapter in our story ushers in a new era in the place which Saint Joseph would have in the life of the Church. The catalyst for this development is the formalization of Saint Joseph's relationship to Carmel—both the Discalced and the Ancient Order of Carmel. A starting point in this process may be found in Gracián's magisterial *Josephina: Summary of the Excellencies of Saint Joseph*, which was simultaneously published in Spanish and in Italian in Rome in 1597, with several translations and many editions thereafter:

> This Order recognizes as the founder of its reform the glorious St. Joseph because it was with his assistance that Mother Teresa carried out this reform, just as the Order of Carmel acknowledges as its founder the most holy Virgin Mary, with whose assistance the Prophet Elijah initiated the religious life of the prophets on Mount Carmel [...]. And not only is the reform of this Order in the present age due to this glorious saint but also the reform of other Orders that has begun in imitation of the reform of Carmel.[57]

Nonetheless, for a time there was uncertainty about the role to be attributed to Saint Joseph in the Teresian reform. However, by the early seventeenth century, veneration of Saint Joseph was recognized as second only to the Virgin Mary and as followed by devotion to the great prophets, Elijah and Elisha, the legendary founders of Carmel. In 1628, Saint Joseph was declared the principal patron of the Discalced Carmelites. This initiative was

---

57 *Just Man*, 242.

given a liturgical dimension in 1680, when the Holy See granted the Discalced Carmelites permission to celebrate the Feast of the Patronage of Saint Joseph on the Third Sunday after Easter, with proper texts for the Mass and Divine Office.[58] The reason for the selection of this particular Sunday was that it was the day stipulated in the Discalced Carmelite Constitutions for when Provincial Chapters were to be held every three years.[59] Being celebrated during the Easter season, the feast was also linked to the paschal glory and joy of the Resurrection, whereas March 19 always falls during the Lenten season.[60]

Also in 1680, the General Chapter of the Carmelites of the Ancient Observance unanimously chose Saint Joseph as the order's principal patron, and not long afterward they also took up the feast of the Patronage. In 1721, the feast was granted an octave. It also quickly spread to many other religious orders and dioceses. By the middle of the nineteenth century, the Feast of the Patronage of Saint Joseph had become widespread, and in 1847 Pope Pius IX extended it to the whole Church. This presaged Saint Joseph's proclamation as Patron of the Universal Church twenty-three years later, on December 8, 1870, which was the theological recognition of the reality already globally celebrated in the Church's liturgy (Figure 19).[61]

---

58 "St. Joseph, Patron of Carmel," 7–8; and Boaga, 45–46. For the original proper texts of the Feast of the Patronage, see Gabriel de la Cruz, OCD, "Los oficios litúrgicos del Patrocinio de San José para los Carmelitas Descalzos de España: Origen, autor y texto," *Estudios Josefinos* 11, no. 21 (1957): 92–115.

59 Luis J. F. Frontela, "El patrocinio de san José sobre el Carmelo Descalzo," *Estudios Josefinos* 74, no. 148 (2020): 195–226, esp. 221.

60 Emilio José Martínez González, OCD, "El patronazgo de San José sobre la Iglesia: Reflexión teológico-espiritual," *Estudios Josefinos* 74, no. 148 (2020): 153–94, esp. 166 (hereafter Martínez González).

61 "St. Joseph, Patron of Carmel," 8–10; Boaga, 45–46; and Larry M. Toschi, OSJ, "Liturgical Feasts of Saint Joseph in the 19th and

Figure 19. *Saint Joseph, Patron of the Universal Church.* London, Richmond upon Thames, Saint Elizabeth of Portugal Church.
Photo: Wikimedia Commons, Fr. James Bradley. August 9, 2016.

The choice of date for this proclamation was not accidental: it was the Solemnity of the Immaculate Conception, as well as the anniversary of the solemn definition of that dogma sixteen years earlier in 1854. By associating the Immaculate

---

20th Centuries," in *Saint Joseph Studies: Papers in English from the Seventh and Eighth International St. Joseph Symposia, Malta 1997 and El Salvador 2001*, ed. Larry M. Toschi, OSJ (Guardian of the Redeemer Books, 2002), 25–58, esp. 36–37 (hereafter Toschi).

Conception with Saint Joseph, Pius IX makes clear that Joseph is second in dignity, intercessory power, and heavenly glory only to the Virgin Mary, to whom he was united in the most sublime and sanctifying marriage possible and by virtue of which he became the earthly father and guardian of Jesus.[62] Echoing Teresa's insistence that the members of the Holy Family are inseparable, Joseph's absolutely unique relationship with Mary and Jesus as the foundation of his preeminence among the saints is henceforth a primary theme in the papal magisterium, being vigorously and fully developed by Pius's immediate successor, Leo XIII, and, more recently, by John Paul II and Francis.[63]

The central panel of our triptych features Giuseppe Rollini's monumental painting of 1893, *Saint Joseph, Patron of the Universal Church*, which he executed for the Saint Joseph altar of the Basilica of the Sacred Heart in Rome (Figure 20).[64] Standing majestically in the center of the composition, Joseph dominates

---

62 Bl. Pope Pius IX, *Quemadmodum Deus: Decree of December 8, 1870 Declaring Saint Joseph "Patron of the Universal Church,"* in Francis L. Filas, SJ, *Joseph: The Man Closest to Jesus. The Complete Life, Theology and Devotional History of St. Joseph*, 2nd printing (St. Paul Editions, 1962), 578–81, esp. 579–80 (hereafter *Quemadmodum Deus*); Daniele Menozzi, "De patron de l'Église universelle à modèle des travailleurs: La dévotion à saint Joseph au XIXe siècle," *Rivista di Storia e Letteratura Religiosa* 56, no. 3 (2020): 559–69, esp. 560–62.

63 See Boniface Hicks, OSB, "Saint Joseph and the Indispensable Role of the Holy Family," *Nova et Vetera*, English edition 20, no. 1 (2022): 61–76.

64 Pius IX had purchased the land for a church to be constructed in honor of Saint Joseph. Although the church was later dedicated instead to the Sacred Heart, the altar and painting of Saint Joseph are a splendid reminder of the church's original intent. See Elizabeth Lev, *The Silent Knight: A History of St. Joseph as Depicted in Art* (Sophia Institute Press, 2021), 174 (hereafter Lev).

Figure 20. Giuseppe Rollini, *Saint Joseph, Patron of the Universal Church*, 1893. Rome, Basilica of the Sacred Heart, Saint Joseph Altar.
Photo: Author.

the pictorial space. He holds his customary attribute of the lily, symbolic of his virginity, and the Christ Child. The Virgin Mary is depicted as the *Mater Dolorosa*, "Sorrowful Mother," who endured her Son's Passion and death on the cross, and whose sorrow is now directed toward the suffering of the Church at this perilous moment in its history. As Mary looks on, a kneeling angel presents Joseph a miniature model of Saint Peter's Basilica, representing the Universal Church. Overhead, an angel holds a scroll with the inscription, *Ite ad Ioseph*, "Go to Joseph." This verbal message is reinforced by the artist's portrayal of the Christ Child, who is the only person in the painting looking directly at the viewer. Holding a small blue orb surmounted with a gold cross signifying His mission as *Salvator Mundi*, "Savior of the World," Jesus tenderly points to Joseph, visually—wordlessly— communicating to the viewer, "Go to Joseph." The dynamic interplay of text and image could not be more poignant.[65]

Rollini's inclusion of the inscription, *Ite ad Joseph*, is not happenstance. Pius IX began his official decree, *Quemadmodum Deus*, proclaiming Saint Joseph "Patron of the Universal Church," by appealing to the comparison between Joseph of Egypt and Joseph of Nazareth, first developed by Saint Bernard of Clairvaux.[66] When seven years of plenty were followed by

---

65 Cf. Lev, 171–81, who discusses Rollini's painting, as well as others of the same subject.

66 *Quemadmodum Deus*, 578. Also see Filas, *Joseph: The Man Closest to Jesus*, 495. The typology of the two Josephs was salient in the liturgy of both the Feast of Saint Joseph (March 19) and of the Patronage (later Solemnity) of Saint Joseph. For March 19, the three lessons of the First Nocturn of Matins were taken from the Old Testament story of Joseph of Egypt (Genesis 39:1–5; 41:37–40; 41:41–44), and the three lessons of the Second Nocturn are from Saint Bernard's sermon on the two Josephs: see *Breviarium Romanum ex decreto Sacrosancti Concilii Tridentini [...], Pars Verna* (Tours: Typis A. Mame et Filiorum, n.d., but likely c. 1930), 817–20

seven years of famine, Pharoah instructed the Egyptians, "Go to Joseph and do whatever he tells you" (Genesis 41:56 *NAB*), for Joseph had made provision to feed Egypt during the famine.

Now the Church makes this counsel its own, as it faces "new and extraordinarily difficult challenges," which included "the ongoing effects of the [French] Revolution and [...] the philosophies that undergirded it," "the dramatic social changes resulting from the Industrial Revolution," and "the intellectual changes emerging from the newly critical approaches to the past, which did not spare sacred texts and sacred traditions."[67] In the midst of these "most troublous times," when "the Church is beset by enemies on every side" and "ungodly men assert that the gates of hell have at length prevailed against her,"[68] the Church turned to Saint Joseph. As the divinely appointed

---

(hereafter *Breviarium Romanum*). For the Patronage/Solemnity of Saint Joseph, the three lessons of the First Nocturn of Matins also narrated the story of Joseph of Egypt (Genesis 39:1–6; 41:37–41; 41:44–49). Moreover, the three lessons of the Second Nocturn of Matins for the second day in the octave of the Patronage/Solemnity were from Bernard's sermon on the two Josephs: see *Breviarium Romanum*, 937–38, 956–57. The Epistle for the Patronage/Solemnity was the dying Jacob's blessing of his son Joseph (Genesis 49:22–26): see *Missale Romanum ex decreto Sacrosancti Concilii Tridentini [...]* (Benziger Brothers, Inc., 1953), 560.

67 John W. O'Malley, *Vatican I: The Council and the Making of the Ultramontane Church* (The Belknap Press of Harvard University Press, 2018), 25. It should also be noted that the context for the selection and liturgical celebration of Saint Joseph's patronage for Carmel as a whole "has always been that of great trial and tribulation, due to both problems within the Order and aggression of the historical, political, and religious circumstances of the time" ("St. Joseph, Patron of Carmel," 9). For fuller treatment of Joseph's proclamation as Patron of the Universal Church in its historical context and beyond, see Martínez González, 153–94.

68 *Quemadmodum Deus*, 580.

protector and guardian of the Holy Family, which was the beginning of the Church, Saint Joseph is the *de facto* Patron of the Universal Church, which "is the continuation of the Body of Christ in history."[69]

The turbulent context for Pius's proclamation of Saint Joseph as Patron of the Universal Church is reflected in Rollini's painting by the artist's use of *chiaroscuro*. The ominous gray clouds in the background suggest the darkness threatening to envelop the Church. However, in the foreground, are the luminous figures of Joseph, the Christ Child, and Mary. *Ite ad Ioseph*, the Church prays, that the protection of Joseph who sheltered "the Light of the World from the encroaching darkness [of] the malice of Herod,"[70] may luminously shine upon it and make it triumphant over the powers of darkness.

Epilogue

To sum up: It is possible to follow an arc from the rich liturgical cult of Saint Joseph in the Carmelite Order of the Ancient Observance; to Saint Joseph's vital formative presence in Saint Teresa's life and reformed Carmel as father, teacher of prayer, and intercessor in every need; to the Carmelite family as a whole giving liturgical expression to its privileged relationship with Saint Joseph by the Feast of the Patronage of Saint Joseph; to this feast becoming widespread outside Carmel and ultimately extended to the Universal Church; and, finally, to Saint Joseph's proclamation as Patron of the Universal Church. Carmelite "veneration of Saint Joseph is not only a devotion or pious practice, but rather […] an integral part of the charis-

---

69   *Patris Corde*, no. 5.
70   Leonard J. DeLorenzo, *Model of Faith: Reflecting on the Litany of Saint Joseph* (Our Sunday Visitor, 2021), 43.

matic heritage of Carmel,"[71] which has overflowed to the benefit and enrichment of the Universal Church.

Foundational to this development at every stage was the lived liturgical experience of Carmel and beyond of the celebration of the Feast of Saint Joseph on March 19 and, subsequently, the Feast of the Patronage (later Solemnity) of Saint Joseph during the Easter season. The former, which celebrates the saint's singular mission and role in salvation history, is the foundation for the latter, which focuses on the continuation of Joseph's mission and role as "the protector which divine Providence has chosen for His Church."[72] Effectively forming a liturgical diptych of, to adopt the words of John Paul II, the "Person and Mission of Saint Joseph in the Life of Christ" and the "Person and Mission of Saint Joseph in the Life of the Church,"[73] these two complementary feasts were celebrated from 1680, with minor modifications, until a half-dozen years before the Second Vatican Council (1962–65).

In the early twentieth century, Pope Saint Pius X refined the Feast of the Patronage in two ways. In 1911, it was renamed the "Solemnity of Saint Joseph, Spouse of the Blessed Virgin Mary, Confessor, Patron of the Universal Church." Then in 1913 the Solemnity was transferred from the Third Sunday after Easter to the Wednesday before the Third Sunday after Easter, while maintaining its octave (Figure 21). The latter was part of Pius's program of liturgical reform, which,

---

71 "St. Joseph, Patron of Carmel," 13.
72 Gaspar Lefebvre, OSB, *Saint Andrew Daily Missal* (E. M. Lohmann Co., 1949), 375 (introductory commentary to the Solemnity of Saint Joseph).
73 These correspond to the two parts of the subtitle of John Paul's apostolic exhortation, *Guardian of the Redeemer: On the Person and Mission of Saint Joseph in the Life of Christ and of the Church*. See note 5 above.

FERIA IV INFRA HEBDOMADAM II POST OCTAVAM PASCHAE

IN SOLEMNITATE
S. JOSEPH SPONSI B.M.V.

Confessoris et Ecclesiæ Universalis Patroni

Duplex I classis cum Octava communi

Introitus Ps. 32, 20-21

Adjútor, et protéctor noster est Dóminus: in eo lætábitur cor nostrum, et in nómine sancto ejus sperávimus, allelúja, allelúja. Ps. 79, 2 Qui regis Israël, inténde: qui dedúcis, velut ovem, Joseph. ℣. Glória Patri. Adjútor.

Oratio

Deus, qui ineffábili providéntia beátum Joseph sanctíssimæ Genitrícis tuæ sponsum elígere dignátus es: præsta, quæsumus; ut, quem protectórem venerámur in terris, intercessórem habére mereámur in cælis: Qui vivis et regnas cum Deo Patre in unitáte Spíritus Sancti Deus: per ómnia sæcula sæculórum.

Léctio libri Génesis
Gen. 49, 22-26

Fílius accréscens Joseph, fílius accréscens, et decórus aspéctu: fíliæ discurrérunt super murum. Sed exasperavérunt eum, et jurgáti sunt, inviderúntque illi habéntes jácula. Sedit in forti arcus ejus, et dissolúta sunt víncula brachiórum et mánuum illíus per manus poténtis Jacob: inde pastor egréssus est, lapis Israël. Deus patris tui erit adjútor tuus, et Omnípotens benedícet tibi, benedictiónibus cæli désuper, benedictiónibus abýssi jacéntis deórsum, benedictiónibus úberum et vulvæ. Benedictiónes patris tui confortátæ sunt benedictiónibus patrum ejus, donec veníret desidérium cóllium æternórum: fiant in cápite Joseph, et in vértice Nazaræi inter fratres suos.

Figure 21. "Solemnity of Saint Joseph, Patron of the Universal Church," from *Missale Romanum ex decreto Sacrosancti Concilii Tridentini […]* (New York: Benziger Brothers, Inc., 1953), 560. Photo: Author.

among other things, moved all feasts, except the Most Holy Trinity, from Sunday to restore priority to the Lord's Day in its own right.[74]

Forty-two years later, a more far-reaching change was made. Saint Joseph's advocation as patron of workers and labor guilds had a long history; however, beginning in the nineteenth century, the popes began to appeal ever more frequently to the saint as a model and patron of the working class. This culminated with Pope Pius XII instituting on May 1, 1955, the Feast of Saint Joseph the Worker in order to Christianize the European secular celebration of labor, May Day, which the Communists exploited for their own purposes.[75] By May 1, 1956, new texts had been promulgated for the Divine Office and Mass for the new feast, whose major theme was that "Joseph's work continues the work of God in creating the world. [...] God, who is Father and worker (*pater, opifex*) making all things, is called upon to help us in our work to imitate St. Joseph, who is also our father and a worker (*pater, opifex*)" (Figure 22).[76] At the same time, the Solemnity of Saint Joseph was suppressed, but the title "Patron of the Universal Church" was preserved liturgically by adding it to March 19. The Discalced Carmelites, who had originated the Feast of the Patronage nearly 300 years earlier, were permitted to keep it in the order's proper calendar, on the third Wednesday after Easter.[77] However, this situation was short-lived.

---

74 See Toschi, 37; and Filas, *Joseph: The Man Closest to Jesus*, 572–73.
75 Toschi, 44–45. The text of the *Acts of Pope Pius XII* instituting the Feast of Saint Joseph the Worker formed the three lessons of the Second Nocturn of Matins for the feast: see *The Roman Breviary: An Approved English Translation in One Volume from the Official Text of the Breviarium Romanum Authorized by the Holy See* (Benziger Brothers, 1964), 852–53.
76 Toschi, 45.
77 Toschi, 37–38.

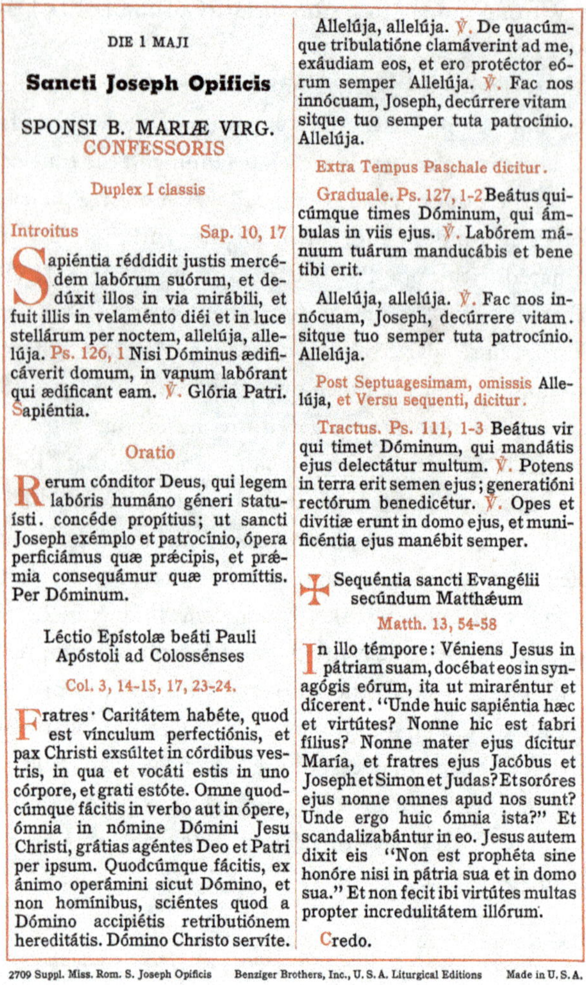

DIE 1 MAJI

Sancti Joseph Opificis

SPONSI B. MARIÆ VIRG.
CONFESSORIS

Duplex I classis

Introitus Sap. 10, 17

Sapiéntia réddidit justis mercédem labórum suórum, et dedúxit illos in via mirábili, et fuit illis in veláménto diéi et in luce stellárum per noctem, allelúja, allelúja. Ps. 126, 1 Nisi Dóminus ædificáverit domum, in vanum labórant qui ædíficant eam. ℣. Glória Patri. Sapiéntia.

Oratio

Rerum cónditor Deus, qui legem labóris humáno géneri statuísti. concéde propítius; ut sancti Joseph exémplo et patrocínio, ópera perficiámus quæ præcipis, et præmia consequámur quæ promíttis. Per Dóminum.

Léctio Epístolæ beáti Pauli Apóstoli ad Colossénses

Col. 3, 14-15, 17, 23-24.

Fratres· Caritátem habéte, quod est vínculum perfectiónis, et pax Christi exsúltet in córdibus vestris, in qua et vocáti estis in uno córpore, et grati estóte. Omne quodcúmque fácitis in verbo aut in ópere, ómnia in nómine Dómini Jesu Christi, grátias agéntes Deo et Patri per ipsum. Quodcúmque fácitis, ex ánimo operámini sicut Dómino, et non homínibus, sciéntes quod a Dómino accipiétis retributiónem hereditátis. Dómino Christo servíte.

Allelúja, allelúja. ℣. De quacúmque tribulatióne clamáverint ad me, exáudiam eos, et ero protéctor eórum semper Allelúja. ℣. Fac nos innócuam, Joseph, decúrrere vitam sitque tuo semper tuta patrocínio. Allelúja.

Extra Tempus Paschale dicitur.

Graduale. Ps. 127, 1-2 Beátus quicúmque times Dóminum, qui ámbulas in viis ejus. ℣. Labórem mánuum tuárum manducábis et bene tibi erit.

Allelúja, allelúja. ℣. Fac nos innócuam, Joseph, decúrrere vitam. sitque tuo semper tuta patrocínio. Allelúja.

Post Septuagesimam, omissis Allelúja, et Versu sequenti, dicitur.

Tractus. Ps. 111, 1-3 Beátus vir qui timet Dóminum, qui mandátis ejus delectátur multum. ℣. Potens in terra erit semen ejus; generatióni rectórum benedicétur. ℣. Opes et divítiæ erunt in domo ejus, et munificéntia ejus manébit semper.

✠ Sequéntia sancti Evangélii secúndum Matthǽum

Matth. 13, 54-58

In illo témpore: Véniens Jesus in pátriam suam, docébat eos in synagógis eórum, ita ut miraréntur et dícerent. "Unde huic sapiéntia hæc et virtútes? Nonne hic est fabri fílius? Nonne mater ejus dícitur María, et fratres ejus Jacóbus et Joseph et Simon et Judas? Et soróres ejus nonne omnes apud nos sunt? Unde ergo huic ómnia ista?" Et scandalizabántur in eo. Jesus autem dixit eis "Non est prophéta sine honóre nisi in pátria sua et in domo sua." Et non fecit ibi virtútes multas propter incredulitátem illórum.

Credo.

2709 Suppl. Miss. Rom. S. Joseph Opificis Benziger Brothers, Inc., U. S. A. Liturgical Editions Made in U. S. A.

Figure 22. "Feast of Saint Joseph the Worker," supplement for the *Missale Romanum* (New York: Benziger Brothers, Inc., 1956). Photo: Author.

The 1969 revised liturgical calendar, approved by Pope Saint Paul VI, ushered in sweeping changes. March 19 was simply designated "Joseph, Husband of Mary," thus removing all liturgical mention of the saint's role as patron of the Church. Enacting a general purification of the calendar by eliminating all mention of patronages in order to leave local devotions to particular calendars, the "blanket application of this principle failed to recognize that St. Joseph's patronage over the Church is in no way limited to particular locations, but is in essence truly universal."[78] The 1969 calendar also reduced the rank of the Feast of Saint Joseph the Worker from the highest to the lowest possible, an optional memorial.[79] Nonetheless, both branches of Carmel were permitted to add "Protector of Our Order" to the title of the feast on March 19, and the Discalced Carmelites upgraded the optional memorial of Saint Joseph the Worker to an obligatory memorial.[80]

Over the years, several petitions have been made to the Holy See to restore the title, "Patron of the Universal Church," to March 19, but all have received negative replies. At the same time, recent popes, particularly John Paul II and Francis, have authoritatively insisted that Joseph's "patronage must be invoked as ever necessary for the Church, not only as a defense against all dangers, but also, and indeed primarily, as an impetus for her renewed commitment to evangelization […] and to re-evangelization."[81] The omission of Joseph's patronage of the universal Church from the liturgical calendar, therefore,

---

78 Toschi, 38. For a full account of the removal of Joseph's title as "Patron of the Universal Church" from the liturgy, see Teófanes Egido, "El patrocinio de san José y su expulsion de la liturgia oficial de la Iglesia," *Estudios Josefinos* 74, no. 148 (2020): 227–61.

79 Toschi, 46.

80 Boaga, 46.

81 *Guardian of the Redeemer*, no. 29.

does not align with the papal magisterium, and it is to be hoped that "eventually [this title will] be given again the liturgical recognition accorded it during such a long period of time."[82]

Catholic writer Mike Aquilina has recently observed that "St. Joseph has not changed, of course. What he was in the New Testament, he has remained through all Christian history: the earthly father of our Savior, the chaste and loving husband of the Virgin Mary, an iconic witness to the dignity of work, and an effective guardian of the Church throughout the world. As devotion develops over time, we can see all of this more clearly."[83]

Within the long view suggested by Aquilina, we have focused on one chapter—spanning nearly five centuries—in the process of seeing more clearly who Saint Joseph is vis-à-vis the Church. Specifically, we have followed the progression from Saint Joseph's privileged place in the Carmelite Order of the Ancient Observance, to his foundational role in Saint Teresa's Carmelite reform, and, finally, to the decisive contribution that both branches of the Carmelite family made to disseminating devotion to Saint Joseph globally, culminating with his proclamation as Patron of the Universal Church. The Church's observance of the Year of Saint Joseph to mark the 150th anniversary of this proclamation is the occasion and the context for the focus of this Second Annual Lecture in Carmelite Studies on Saint Joseph. Today as yesterday, Carmel's venerable tradition of prayerful reflection on Saint Joseph, firm confidence in his intercessory power in every need, and unwavering celebration of his patronage and paternity of the order

---

82 Toschi, 39.
83 Mike Aquilina, "Getting to Know Joseph: The Church's Appreciation for the Head of the Holy Family Has Developed over Millennia," *Columbia Magazine* (March 2021): 16.

is an indispensable resource and model for the Church in its continuing journey of discovery of the person and mission of Saint Joseph.

> Hail, Guardian of the Redeemer,
> Spouse of the Blessed Virgin Mary.
> To you God entrusted His only Son;
> in you Mary placed her trust;
> with you Christ became man.
> Blessed Joseph, to us too,
> show yourself a father
> and guide us in the path of life.
> Obtain for us grace, mercy and courage,
> and defend us from every evil. Amen.[84]

Joseph F. Chorpenning, OSFS

---

84 *Patris Corde*, no.7.

ST. JOSEPH,
PATRON OF CARMEL

*A Letter from the Prior General, O.Carm. and
Superior General, OCD to the Carmelite Family
on the occasion of the 150th anniversary of the proclamation
of St. Joseph as Patron of the Universal Church*

This year, 2020, we celebrated the feast of St. Joseph in the full throes of a pandemic that forced us to remain in our own homes. Because of that, we felt the need even more to turn to that just and faithful man who knew the meaning of hardship, exile, and worries about tomorrow but did not lose heart, continuing to believe and hope [in] God, from whom he had received a very unique mission: he was to take care of Mary

---

Editor's Note: This text has been lightly edited to bring the spelling, punctuation, etc., into greater conformity with American usage.

and the child Jesus, the family of Nazareth, the embryo of the new family that God was giving to the world. Pope Francis, preaching in Santa Marta, reminded us of some of the qualities of St. Joseph: the man of clear and practical vision, capable of doing his work with precision and professional skill, and one who at the same time penetrated the mystery of God, beyond all that was familiar to him or was under his control, and in the presence of which he kneels and adores.[1]

It does us good to think about St. Joseph, to meditate on him as one whom our tradition has recognized as a patron and a model of Carmelite life. It is something we want to do together, as a Carmelite family, O.Carm. and OCD, because in our veneration of St. Joseph, and in our constant reference to him, we find one of the most precious aspects of our common heritage and spirituality. This year has the added motivation of a significant anniversary, namely, the proclamation of St. Joseph as Patron of the Universal Church, by Pope Pius IX, on the 8th of December 1870, 150 years ago.

The Place of St. Joseph in Carmel

The veneration of St. Joseph is an integral part of our Christian formation, tradition, and culture. We are so accustomed to placing St. Joseph alongside Jesus and Mary that we tend to think that the church has always attributed to him, whose life was one of intimacy with the mystery of the Incarnation, the dignity and the honors that we normally associate with him; but in reality, it was not always so. In the first millennium, the traces of a theological reflection on St. Joseph, or of any particular homage given to him, are very rare. It was only with the advent of the mendicant orders that devotion to

---

[1] Pope Francis, "Homily," Santa Marta, March 19, 2020.

St. Joseph began to develop. In addition to the work of the French theologian, Jean Gerson, a decisive contribution was given by the Franciscans and by the Carmelites.

For Carmelites, interest in St. Joseph was a natural offshoot of its fundamental Marian orientation. Every member of the wider family of Mary (her parents, Joachim and Anne, the secondary protectors of Carmel, and his alleged sisters and brothers, Mary of James and Mary of Salome) were the recipients of particular attention in Carmel. In that context, Joseph, Mary's spouse, could not be ignored. Pious medieval legends, in order to underline the close link with the family of Nazareth, Jesus, Mary and Joseph, and based perhaps on the Apocryphal Gospel of Pseudo-Matthew, make references to visits that the Holy Family made to the sons of the prophets, the descendants of the prophet Elijah, living on Mount Carmel. Others speak about a presumed visit that the Holy Family made on their return from Egypt.[2] This connection must have looked so strong in the Church that some of the ancient authors, like the Benedictine abbot, Giovanni Tritemio, thought that perhaps the veneration of St. Joseph in the Latin Church may well have been brought by the Carmelite hermits on their return to Europe.[3] This idea, which is no longer accepted, is one that we find in the writings of Pope Benedict XIV, who suggested that the veneration of St. Joseph in the liturgy began

---

2   These pious legends inspired important works of art, e.g., paintings from the end of the 15th century that hang today in the Cathedral Museum in Frankfurt-am-Main.

3   Leone di San Gioacchino, *Il culto di San Giuseppe e l'Ordine del Carmelo* (Barcelona, 1905), 48. For the history of the development, see Emanuele Boaga, "Giuseppe, santo e sposo della BVM," in *Dizionario Carmelitano*, ed. Emanuele Boaga and Luigi Borriello (Città Nuova, 2008), 443–46.

with the Carmelites.⁴ What is certain is that devotion to St. Joseph among Carmelites had liturgical overtones from the very beginning. In later times, and right up to the present day, we find also a Eucharistic dimension in Carmelite devotion to St. Joseph, as the one who held in his hands the bread of life, our spiritual food and drink.

In truth, it is impossible to say exactly when people began to celebrate the feast of St. Joseph in Carmelite churches. In all probability, as early as the 14th century, there was strong local devotion, but by the 15th century we begin to see a Mass and a Divine Office proper to St. Joseph. The Flemish Carmelite, Arnold Bostius, in 1476, stated that Carmelites had a solemn celebration of his feast.⁵ The proper of the liturgy in honor of St. Joseph in the Carmelite tradition is thought by historians and liturgists to be [the] first monument of the Latin Church to the dignity of St. Joseph.

The ancient liturgy celebrates St. Joseph as the first among his contemporaries in Nazareth, the one chosen by Divine Wisdom to be the Spouse of the Virgin Mary, so that the Son of God might enter the world with honor but without fanfare. Carmelite preachers insisted that just as Mary the Virgin conceived the Incarnate Word in her womb through the work of the Holy Spirit, so Joseph, through the work of the same Holy Spirit, conceived the Word through contemplation, and became the father of Jesus on this earth.⁶ The liturgy celebrated

---

4   Benedict XIV, *De Serv. Dei beatif.,* I/iv, 11; I/xx, 17. [*De Servorum Dei Beatificatione et Beatorum Canonizatione,* 1765]

5   Bartolomé Xiberta, "Flores josefinas en la liturgia carmelitana antigua," *Estudios Josefinos* 18 (1963–1964): 301–19.

6   Christoval de Avendaño, *Tomo primero sobre los evangelios de la quaresma, predicados en la corte de Madrid …* (Barcelona: Sebastian y Iayme Matevad, 1630), 158–59.

the nuptial union between Joseph and Mary the Virgin, and presented him as the protector of her virginity and of the life of the incarnate Son of God. With the sensitivity that is typical of the Carmelite contemplative charism, the ancient liturgy celebrated the purity of the Blessed Virgin and of St. Joseph, by highlighting their openness to God, which made it possible for them to welcome the mystery of the Incarnation. Formed by this liturgical spirituality, St. Mary Magdalene de' Pazzi would see Joseph's protection as a consequence of his purity: "In paradise Joseph's purity joins with the purity of Mary, and in that exchange of splendor, Joseph's purity shines a light on the even greater glory and splendor of Mary's purity. Saint Joseph is in the middle of Jesus and Mary as a resplendent star, and he takes particular care of our monastery because we are under the care of the Virgin Mary."[7]

St. Joseph is presented in Carmel's ancient liturgy as the virginal spouse of Mary, united to her through a real marriage, in which his authority as a spouse, protector, and father is seen in his constant service. Moreover, St. Joseph is presented in his obedience to God. He is the just one, the worthy master of the house of the Lord, to whom a great responsibility is entrusted, that of giving a name to the child that is born. He gave him the divine name announced by the angel, the name Jesus. By doing this, Joseph became the first one to announce that in the child of Nazareth we are saved by God. In that same ancient liturgy, we can detect a wealth of Carmelite spirituality under the image of St. Joseph: 1) *puritas cordis* [purity of heart] that makes it possible to have a vision of God; 2) union with Mary;

---

7   Santa Maria Maddalena de' Pazzi, "Vigesimo secondo colloquio," in *I Colloqui: Tutte le opere ... dai manoscritti originali*, ed. Claudio Catena (Fulvio Nardoni, 1961), 237–38.

and 3) the fruitfulness of the mystical life understood in terms of the conception and birth of the incarnate Word in the soul that is pure. St. Joseph for that reason is celebrated as the image and reflection of the Carmelite mystical life in God.

Saint Teresa and Saint Joseph

As the heir of a rich tradition of veneration and devotion to St. Joseph in Carmel, St. Teresa of Jesus would give more breadth and depth to the tradition, to the great benefit of Carmel and of the universal church. Indeed, it is undeniable that more than any other, Teresa of Jesus made devotion to Joseph one of the elements that characterizes the spiritual identity of Carmel. Her encounter with St. Joseph came about in one of the darkest periods in her life. She was about twenty-five years old. She had been suffering from a painful and endless illness, and the doctors had not only not cured her but made her worse. She was paralyzed and worn out, both physically and psychologically. She felt that she was alone, without anybody to help her, when as if she felt something inside pushing her, she turned to St. Joseph as her "lord and father" (*Life* 6.6; 33.12). For the rest of her life, Joseph would remain for her and her work as the custodian and protector, taking her out of every difficulty that came her way. From being only a personal devotion, her devotion to Joseph would become in time a feature of the Teresian Reform centered on friendship with Jesus Christ. Just as Joseph watched over the relationship between Jesus and Mary, defending it from dangers from outside and protecting the home where they dwelt, likewise, he would watch over the Carmels that, just like the family of Nazareth, were intended to be places in which the humanity of Jesus would find a home, and Carmelites would live only for that end. For this reason, Joseph is not only a patron, but also the master of all who practice prayer (*Life* 6.8), because there is no one who knows more than he what it means to live a life of intimacy with Jesus and Mary, because of the many years he lived with them and the way in which he made possible their life as a family in Nazareth. It is no surprise therefore that ten out of the fifteen Carmelite monasteries that Teresa herself founded bore the name of St. Joseph.

St. Joseph was so much a presence in the founding activities of Teresa (every time she travelled she brought with her a statue of St. Joseph) that he began to be known as the "Founder" of the Teresian Carmel.[8] We should understand by that that he truly helped her in the founding of the Carmelite monasteries of the reform. It is certain, however, that alongside the traditional figure of the Prophet Elijah, there was now a place for St. Joseph, and this caused some questioning, as to which of these should be considered the principal patron and founder after the Blessed Virgin Mary.[9] It is significant that in a letter to Fr. Gracián, Teresa in trying to decide what name should be given to the college that they were establishing in Salamanca, wrote "It is an excellent idea to name this college

---

8   [Jerónimo] Gracián, in a well-known passage from his work *Josefina* (1597), reached the point of stating that: "This [Discalced Carmelite] Order recognizes as the founder of its reform the glorious St. Joseph because it was with his assistance that Mother Teresa carried out this reform, just as the Order of Carmel acknowledges as its founder the most holy Virgin Mary, with whose assistance the prophet Elijah initiated the religious life of the prophets on Mount Carmel"; see *Just Man, Husband of Mary, Guardian of Christ: An Anthology of Readings from Jerónimo Gracián's Summary of the Excellencies of St. Joseph (1597)*, trans. and ed. Joseph F. Chorpenning (Saint Joseph's University Press, 1995), 242.

9   Fortunato de Jesús Sacramentado, "San José en el Carmen Descalzo español en su primer siglo," *Estudios Josefinos* 18 (1963–1964): 367.

[after] St. Joseph" (Letter, May 22, 1578)[10] but [ultimately] the college will be called after Saint Elijah. The following year, in 1579, St. John of the Cross gave the name of St. Joseph to the college in Baeza, which made the college in Baeza the first male foundation that was dedicated to St. Joseph. The title, however, lasted only two years. From March 1581 onwards the college would be known as the college of St. Basil, one of the great fathers of the Church. It is clear to us that there was still some uncertainty around the role to be attributed to the carpenter of Nazareth in the Teresian reform of the Carmelites. Things became clearer a quarter of a century later when, in his *Instruction for Novices*, Fr. Giovanni di Gesù Maria explained that veneration of St. Joseph is second only to the Blessed Virgin and is followed by devotion to the great prophets, Elijah and Elisha, the "founders of our Order" (*Istruzione dei novizi*, III, cap. 4, 29–30).[11]

The Patronage of Saint Joseph

One of the characteristic thoughts of Teresa was that while other saints are destined by God to help in certain kinds of need, St. Joseph has a kind of universal mandate, to assist in any kind of need, material or spiritual (*Life* 6.6). It is on

---

10 Editor's Note: Quoted from *The Collected Letters of St. Teresa of Ávila,* trans. Kieran Kavanaugh, vol. 2 (ICS Publications, 2007), 76. In this edition the quotation is found in Letter 247, paragraph 7.

11 Editor's Note: See also the English adaptation of this work, John of Jesus and Mary, *Instruction of Novices* (Loughrea, Ireland: M. S. Kelly & Co., 1925), 246: "After the glorious Virgin Mary, Novices should hold her most worthy spouse Saint Joseph in the highest veneration. And indeed he well deserves it, on account of his exalted dignity, and the benefits he has bestowed on us."

this conviction that the feast of the patronage of St. Joseph was founded, in a way that was typically Carmelite. In the year 1628, the intermediate General Chapter of the Spanish congregation of the Discalced Carmelites declared St. Joseph as the principal patron of the Discalced Order. The initiative of celebrating the feast of the patronage of St. Joseph may be attributed to the Discalced Carmelite Juan de la Concepción (1625–1700), who was the first Provincial of the Province of Catalonia and after that Superior General of the Spanish Congregation. He obtained from the General Chapter of 1679 the approval of the feast of the patronage of St. Joseph, the liturgical texts for which were composed by another Catalan Discalced Carmelite, Juan de San José (1642–1718). The Congregation of Rites, after a comprehensive rewriting of the texts by Cardinal Casanate, approved them on the 6th of April, 1680. The feast of St. Joseph's Patronage was set for the third Sunday after Easter, the day on which normally General and Provincial Chapters were convoked. Very soon after that the feast was taken up by the Carmelites of the Ancient Observance and it was celebrated under the title, *De Patrocinio S. Joseph Confessoris, Protectoris, et Patroni nostrae Religionis*.[12] Already, for a long time, the terms "protector" and/or "patron" were used without distinction to refer to St. Joseph. Very quickly this celebration spread to other orders and religious congregations, up until the time of the proclamation of his patronage of the universal church.

The context of the proclamation and the liturgical celebration of the patronage of St. Joseph for Carmel as a whole has always been that of great trial and tribulation, due to both problems within the Order and aggression of the historical,

---

12 See, for example, *Missale Fratrum Ordinis Beatissimae Virginis Mariae de Monte Carmelo* (Rome, 1759), 350.

political, and religious circumstances of the time. Carmel, in those days, was experiencing great difficulty in its efforts to preserve its own identity and its values. It should be noted that as part of the renewal movements operating within the Carmelite Order, there was a proliferation of devotional writings about St. Joseph that represented particular forms of expression of the kind of piety that warms the heart and gives impetus to the spiritual life. There were several Carmelite authors and preachers who worked untiringly in spreading devotion to Joseph and in promoting his patronage. Worthy of mention, Raffaele il Bavaro who wrote *Istoria di San Giuseppe* in 1723, in which he exhorted his readers who loved Jesus and Mary, to also love Joseph as one who was loved by both of them.[13] Giuseppe Maria Sardi may be considered the great propagator of the patronage of St. Joseph, not only for the Order, but also for Christian parents and others who found in him a model of holiness.[14] It was not without reason that Joseph came to be known among Carmelites as the best of teachers and was held to be the protector and patron especially of those who are overburdened or who have lost their way in trying to follow Jesus Christ.

On the 10th of September 1847, with the decree of the Congregation for Rites, *Inclytus Patriarcha Joseph*, Pope Pius IX, at a time of great tribulation, extended to the whole church the feast of the patronage of St. Joseph, to be celebrated on the Third Sunday of Easter. For the liturgy of the Mass, and the Divine Office, the texts used at that time by the Carmelites were adopted,

---

13 Raffaele Maria Bavaro, *Istoria di San Giuseppe* (Naples: Antonio Abri, 1723), 612; *Vita di San Giuseppe o sia Ristretto della sua Istoria ed Esercizi di Devozione per fruttuosamente venerare il medesimo Santo …* (Antonio Abri, 1724).

14 Giuseppi Maria Sardi (Venato), "Discorso sopra il Padrocinio di San Giuseppe Sposo di Maria," in *Sermoni* (Venice: Lorenzo Rivan Monti, 1742), 213–21.

with some modifications. It was the first gesture by Pius IX in honoring St. Joseph, and he was not yet one full year in office. It was due to his great devotion to the father of Jesus. At the time of convocation of the First Vatican Council, the Pope received a number of requests to increase even more the veneration of St. Joseph, especially by making him the patron of the universal church. The council, which was interrupted unexpectedly in September 1870, did not allow enough time for the request to be granted. Therefore, on the 8th of December of that same year, Pius IX decided upon the solemn proclamation through a decree of the Congregation for Rites *Quemadmodum Deus*.

The feast of the patronage of St. Joseph was transferred in 1913 to Wednesday of the third week after Easter, and then in 1956 it was replaced by the memorial in honor of St. Joseph the Worker, to be celebrated on the 1st of May. Nevertheless, the Discalced Carmelites, with the approval of their liturgical calendar in 1957, were permitted to celebrate the feast of the patronage of St. Joseph, as "the protector and patron of our Order."

Saint Joseph, Patron of Carmel Worldwide

The reform of the liturgy that followed the Second Vatican Council brought, among other things, a notable simplification of the liturgical calendar. In the calendar approved on the 14th of February 1969, the title "protector of the universal church" disappeared from the principal feast of St. Joseph, celebrated on the 19th of March. Of course, it was not abolished, but it was thought that it would be better to hold on to only the biblical title of "spouse of the Virgin Mary," giving the individual bishops' conferences and religious families the freedom to add other titles. Following the instruction of the Congregation for Divine Worship on particular calendars

(29th of June 1969), the solemnity of the patronage of St. Joseph was removed also from the calendar of the Discalced Carmelites. The General Definitory (OCD) decided then to transfer the title of "protector of our Order" to the 19th of March solemnity. Similarly, it was decided that the optional memorial of St. Joseph the Worker should be celebrated throughout the whole Order.[15] These decisions, it would seem, were very quickly forgotten. While the title, "protector of our Order" was kept in the liturgy of the Carmelites of the Ancient Observance, it disappeared very quickly from the liturgy of the Discalced Carmelites, given that in the particular calendar of the Order, neither the solemnity nor the memorial of St. Joseph appeared. Nevertheless, in the post-conciliar constitutions of both Orders there is continued reference to St. Joseph as their protector (Const. O.Carm., 91; Const. OCD, 52). By this fact we may recognize an important element of unity in the Carmelite family as a whole, that perhaps we have not sufficiently considered or appreciated.

Today's World

We are living now in a period in which the church is not so concerned with defending itself from an outside enemy but seeks to recognize its mission of giving authentic witness to the truth of the Gospel. Thus, in a world where there is need for "concreteness and the sense of mystery,"[16] in a world in

---

15 Cfr. "Normae de calendario liturgico OCD pro anno 1970" (approved in the 128th session of the General Definitory, July 18, 1969), in *Ordo Divini Officii recitandi missaeque celebrandae iuxta calendarium romanum ac proprium Carmelitarum Discalceatorum [...] pro anno Domini 1970*, [Rome: Casa generalizia OCD] 1969, 29–32.

16 Pope Francis, "Homily," Santa Marta, March 19, 2020.

which we tend to flee from the bonds of stable relationships and commitments and to revert to a kind of sterile narcissism, Joseph shows us the way of self-denial, daily responsibility, the silent dedication to the care and growth of family. Any father of a family will want to heal the wounds of his own home. Our patron helps us to see the need to heal the wounds of humanity, and the wounds of the church. There is no church, there is no Carmel without people who, forgetting themselves, work day and night to give others a sure foundation in which they can trust. These people work away from the limelight, bearing in their own hearts all their own concerns and anxieties, very often not seeing the fruits or even seeing the goal, trusting only in the One from whom their paternity comes and takes its name (Eph. 3:14–15). These are the people who will always find in St. Joseph their patron and model, "their father and lord."

The Word came to Joseph in a dream, which we may understand as his prayer, his interiority. We might say that every Carmel is a place of dreams: prayer is like a dream, that has within it a secret message. A Carmelite community is a group of people that dreams of making of its own home a new Jerusalem, people who share the dream of the prophet for a better world, people who allow themselves to be captured every day by the dream of salvation. In listening every day to the Word of Salvation, we are conformed to Christ in his obedience and in his desire to serve, as the one who did not come to be served, but to serve, as one who found in small children the example of how [we] must be if we want to enter the kingdom of God. Carmelites, like St. Joseph, know the dream and keep alight the flame of hope that shines for the new world promised to those who are attentive to the word of God, because God will make all things new.

St. Joseph protects Carmel, not only because he protects it from hostile attack and from every adversity,[17] but also because he helps Carmel to remain firm in the simplicity and profundity of its identity. With his being just he points the way that we must follow and the goal for which we must strive. In this sense, there is no doubt that our veneration of St. Joseph is not only a devotion or pious practice, but rather a life plan, that is, an integral part of the charismatic heritage of Carmel. Together with Mary, Joseph is the Gospel icon in which we Carmelites may see and understand what it means to live "in allegiance to Jesus Christ" [*Carmelite Rule,* 2]. It is right then that we continue to turn to him as our father and patron, but also as a faithful friend and reliable guide in our following in the footsteps of Jesus.

As the world continues to deal with COVID-19, we unite in prayer for the doctors and nurses, for medical researchers, and for all who have fallen victim to this pandemic and for the families who are in mourning for the loss of loved ones. May Joseph, our protector, protect each one of us, and with the tender love of God, spread his protection throughout the whole world.

Fraternally in Carmel,

P. Míčeál O'Neill, O.Carm.
Prior General

P. Saverio Cannistrà, OCD
Superior General

---

17 Prayer to St. Joseph by Pope Leo XIII at the end of the encyclical, *Quamquam pluries.*

Bibliography

Álvarez, Tomás, OCD. "San José." In *Diccionario de Santa Teresa*, edited by Tomás Álvarez, 663–69. 3rd edition. Grupo Editorial Fonte—Editorial Monte Carmelo, 2017.

Álvarez, Tomás, OCD. *St. Teresa of Avila: 100 Themes on Her Life and Work*. Translated by Kieran Kavanaugh, OCD. ICS Publications, 2011.

Aquilina, Mike. "Getting to Know Joseph: The Church's Appreciation for the Head of the Holy Family Has Developed over Millennia." *Columbia Magazine* (March 2021): 14–16.

Avendaño, Christoval de. *Tomo primero sobre los evangelios de la quaresma, predicados en la corte de Madrid …* Barcelona: Sebastian y Iayme Matevad, 1630.

Barry, Paul de. *La dévotion à saint Joseph*. 4th edition. Liege, 1642.

Bavaro, Raffaele Maria. *Istoria di San Giuseppe*. Naples: Antonio Abri, 1723.

Bavaro, Raffaele Maria. *Vita di San Giuseppe o sia Ristretto della sua Istoria ed Esercizi di Devozione per fruttuosamente venerare il medesimo Santo …* Naples: Antonio Abri, 1724.

Binet, Étienne. *Le tableau des diverses faveurs faites à saint Joseph*. Paris, 1634.

Boaga, Emanuele, O.Carm. *Celebrating the Saints of Carmel: A Commentary on the Carmelite Proper of the Mass and Liturgy of the Hours*. Translated by Solomon Wright. Edizioni Carmelitane, 2010.

Boaga, Emanuele, O.Carm. "Giuseppe, santo e sposo della BVM." In *Dizionario Carmelitano*, edited by Emanuele Boaga and Luigi Borriello, 443–46. Città Nuova, 2008.

Breviarium Romanum ex decreto Sacrosancti Concilii Tridentini […], Pars Verna. Tours: Typis A. Mame et Filiorum, n.d., but likely c. 1930.

Carruthers, Mary. *The Craft of Thought: Meditation, Rhetoric, and the Making of Images, 400–1200*. Cambridge University Press, 1998.

Chorpenning, Joseph F., OSFS. "Bernardino de Laredo's *Treatise on the Mysteries of St. Joseph* and the Evangelization of Mexico." In *The Mystical Gesture: Essays on Medieval and Early Modern Spiritual Culture in Honor of Mary E. Giles*, edited by Robert Boenig, 67–77. Ashgate, 2000.

Chorpenning, Joseph F., OSFS. "Icon of Family and Religious Life: The Historical Development of the Holy Family Devotion." In *The Holy Family as Prototype of the Civilization of Love: Images from the Viceregal Americas*, edited by Joseph F. Chorpenning, OSFS, 3–39. Saint Joseph's University Press, 1996.

Chorpenning, Joseph F., OSFS. "St. Joseph as Guardian Angel, Artisan, and Contemplative: Christophorus Blancus's Engravings for the *Summary of the Excellencies of St. Joseph* (1597)." In Chorpenning, *Joseph of Nazareth Through the Centuries*, 103–36.

Chorpenning, Joseph F., OSFS, ed. *Joseph of Nazareth Through the Centuries*. Saint Joseph's University Press, 2011.

Cruz, Gabriel de la, OCD. "Los oficios litúrgicos del Patrocinio de San José para los Carmelitas Descalzos de España: Origen, autor y texto." *Estudios Josefinos* 11, no. 21 (1957): 92–115.

d'Ailly, Pierre. "The Twelve Honors Which God Bestowed on St. Joseph." Translated by Robert F. McNamara. *St. Joseph Lillies* 34, no. 1 (1945): 22–25.

DeLorenzo, Leonard J. *Model of Faith: Reflecting on the Litany of Saint Joseph*. Our Sunday Visitor, 2021.

de' Pazzi, Santa Maria Maddalena. "Vigesimo secondo colloquio." In *I Colloqui: Tutte le opere … dai manoscritti originali*. Edited by Claudio Catena. Fulvio Nardoni, 1961.

Dompnier, Bernard. "Thérèse d'Avila et la dévotion française à saint Joseph au XVIIe siècle." *Revue d'Histoire de l'Église de France* 90 (2004): 175–90.

Donohoe, Livinus, OCD. *The Prayer of the Holy Family*. Carmelite Book Service, 2008, reprint 2009.

Doze, André. *Discovering Saint Joseph*. Translated by Florestine Audett, RJM. St Pauls, 1991.

Egido, Teófanes. "El patrocinio de san José y su expulsion de la liturgia official de la Iglesia." *Estudios Josefinos* 74, no. 148 (2020): 227–61.

Eire, Carlos. *The Life of Saint Teresa of Avila: A Biography*. Lives of Great Religious Books. Princeton University Press, 2019.

Faesen, Rob, SJ. "The Grand Silence of St. Joseph: Devotion to St. Joseph and the Seventeenth-Century Crisis of Mysticism in the Jesuit Order." In Chorpenning, *Joseph of Nazareth Through the Centuries*, 137–50.

Filas, Francis L., SJ. *Joseph: The Man Closest to Jesus. The Complete Life, Theology and Devotional History of St. Joseph*. 2nd printing. St. Paul Editions, 1962.

Francis. "Homily." Santa Marta. March 19, 2020.

Francis. *Patris Corde / With a Father's Heart: Apostolic Letter on the 150th Anniversary of the Proclamation of Saint Joseph as Patron of the Universal Church.* Vatican translation (by Helen Crombie). Vatican City: Libreria Editrice Vaticana, 2021.

Frontela, Luis J. F. "El patrocinio de san José sobre el Carmelo Descalzo." *Estudios Josefinos* 74, no. 148 (2020): 195–226.

Gauthier, Roland, CSC. "[Saint Joseph] dans l'histoire de la spiritualité." In *Dictionnaire de spiritualité*, vol. 8, 1308–21. Beauchesne, 1974.

Gisbert de Mesa, Teresa. "Gaspar Miguel de Berrío (Bolivian, 1706–c. 1762), *The Patronage of Saint Joseph*." In *The Arts in Latin America 1492–1820*, organized by Joseph J. Rishel with Suzanne Stratton-Pruitt, 443. Philadelphia Museum of Art / Yale University Press, 2006.

Gracián, Jerónimo. *Just Man, Husband of Mary, Guardian of Christ: An Anthology of Readings from Jerónimo Gracián's "Summary of the Excellencies of St. Joseph" (1597).* Translated and edited, with an introductory essay and commentary, by Joseph F. Chorpenning, OSFS. 2nd edition. Saint Joseph's University Press, 1995.

Hahn, Cynthia. "'Joseph Will Perfect, Mary Enlighten and Jesus Save Thee': The Holy Family as Marriage Model in the Mérode Triptych." *Art Bulletin* 68, no. 1 (1986): 54–66.

Hicks, Boniface, OSB. "Saint Joseph and the Indispensable Role of the Holy Family." *Nova et Vetera*, English edition 20, no. 1 (2022): 61–76.

Huizinga, Johan. *Autumntide of the Middle Ages: A Study of the Forms of Life and Thought of the Fourteenth and Fifteenth Centuries in France and the Low Countries.* Translated by Diane Webb. Edited by Graeme Small and Anton van der Lem. Leiden University Press, 2020.

Jacquinot, Jean. *La gloire de saint Joseph*. Dijon, 1644.

John of Jesus and Mary. *Instruction of Novices*. M. S. Kelly & Co., 1925.

John Paul II. *Redemptoris Custos / Guardian of the Redeemer: On the Person and Mission of Saint Joseph in the Life of Christ and of the Church*. Apostolic Exhortation. August 15, 1989. Vatican translation. United States Catholic Conference, 1989.

Knipping, John B. *Iconography of the Counter Reformation in the Netherlands: Heaven on Earth*. 2 vols. B. de Graaf / A. W. Sijthoff, 1974.

Lefebvre, Gaspar, OSB. *Saint Andrew Daily Missal*. E. M. Lohmann Co., 1949.

Lev, Elizabeth. *The Silent Knight: A History of St. Joseph as Depicted in Art*. Sophia Institute Press, 2021.

Martínez González, Emilio José, OCD. "El patronazgo de San José sobre la Iglesia: Reflexión teológico-espiritual." *Estudios Josefinos* 74, no. 148 (2020): 153–94.

McGuire, Brian Patrick. "Becoming a Father and a Husband: St. Joseph in Bernard of Clairvaux and Jean Gerson." In Chorpenning, *Joseph of Nazareth Through the Centuries*, 49–61.

McGuire, Brian Patrick. *Jean Gerson and the Last Medieval Reformation*. Pennsylvania State University Press, 2005.

McGuire, Brian Patrick. "When Jesus Did the Dishes: The Transformation of Late Medieval Spirituality." In *The Making of Christian Communities in Late Antiquity and the Middle Ages*, edited by Mark F. Williams, 131–52. Anthem Press, 2005.

Menozzi, Daniele. "De patron de l'Église universelle à modèle des travailleurs: La dévotion à saint Joseph au XIXe siècle." *Rivista di Storia e Letteratura Religiosa* 56, no. 3 (2020): 559–69.

Missale Fratrum Ordinis Beatissimae Virginis Mariae de Monte Carmelo. Rome, 1759.

Missale Romanum ex decreto Sacrosancti Concilii Tridentini [...]. Benziger Brothers, Inc., 1953.

Moreno Cuadro, Fernando. "Diseños de Abraham van Diepenbeeck para 'Les peintures sacrees du Temple du Carmel.'" *BSAA arte* 79 (2013): 157–81.

Moreno Cuadro, Fernando. *Iconografía de Santa Teresa, Vol. 3: De las visiones a la vida cotidiana*. Grupo Editorial Fonte—Editorial Monte Carmelo, 2018.

Morris, Michael, OP. *Regina Coeli: Art and Essays on the Blessed Virgin Mary*. Magnificat, 2016.

Noye, Irénée. "Famille (Dévotion à la Sainte Famille)." In *Dictionnaire de spiritualité*, vol. 5, 84–93. Beauchesne, 1964.

Ordo Divini Officii recitandi missaeque celebrandae iuxta calendarium romanum ac proprium Carmelitarum Discalceatorum [...] pro anno Domini 1970. Casa generalizia OCD, 1969.

O'Malley, John W. *Vatican I: The Council and the Making of the Ultramontane Church*. The Belknap Press of Harvard University Press, 2018.

O'Neill, Míċeál, and Saverio Cannistrà. "St. Joseph, Patron of Carmel." *Mount Carmel: A Review of the Spiritual Life* 69, no. 1 (January–March 2021): 1–13.

Ong, Walter J., SJ. *The Presence of the Word: Some Prolegomena for Cultural and Religious History*. Yale University Press, 1967.

Pius IX. *Quemadmodum Deus: Decree of December 8, 1870 Declaring Saint Joseph "Patron of the Universal Church."* In Francis L. Filas, SJ, *Joseph: The Man Closest to Jesus*, 578–81.

Ridderbos, Bernhard. "Choices and Intentions in the Mérode Altarpiece." *Journal of Historians of Netherlandish Art* 14, no. 1 (2022): 1–43.

The Roman Breviary: An Approved English Translation in One Volume from the Official Text of the Breviarium Romanum Authorized by the Holy See. Benziger Brothers, 1964.

Ros García, Salvador. "El carisma del Carmelo vivido e interpretado por santa Teresa." In *La recepción de los místicos Teresa de Jesús y Juan de la Cruz: Ávila, 20–26 de septiembre de 1996*, edited by Salvador Ros García, 537–72. Ediciones Universidad Pontificia, 1997.

San Gioacchino, Leone di. *Il culto di San Giuseppe e l'Ordine del Carmelo*. Barcelona, 1905.

San Joaquín, León de. *El culto de San José y la Orden del Carmen*. Juan Gili, 1905.

Sardi (Venato), Giuseppi Maria. *Sermoni*. Venice: Lorenzo Rivan Monti, 1742.

Schapiro, Meyer. "*Muscipula Diaboli*: The Symbolism of the Mérode Altarpiece." *Art Bulletin* 27, no. 3 (1945): 182–87.

Schapiro, Meyer. "A Note on the Mérode Altarpiece." *Art Bulletin* 41, no. 4 (1959): 327–28.

Sebastián Macías, Facundo. "Hagiography as a Platform for Internal Catholic Debate in Early Modern Europe: Francisco de Ribera's *La vida de la Madre Teresa de Jesus* (1590) and the Defense of a Contemplative Way Inside the Jesuit Order." *Church History* 89, no. 2 (2020): 288–306.

Secretary General of the Discalced Carmelite Nuns. "Saint Joseph: Founder and Father of the Teresian Carmel." In *Saint Joseph and the Third Millennium: Traditional Themes and Contemporary Issues*, edited by Michael D. Griffin, OCD, 305–30. Teresian Charism Press, 1999.

Teresa of Ávila. *The Collected Works of St. Teresa of Ávila*. 3 vols. Translated by Kieran Kavanaugh, OCD, and Otilio Rodríguez, OCD. ICS Publications, 1976–1986.

Toschi, Larry M., OSJ, "Liturgical Feasts of Saint Joseph in the 19th and 20th Centuries." In *Saint Joseph Studies: Papers in English from the Seventh and Eighth International St. Joseph Symposia, Malta 1997 and El Salvador 2001*, edited by Larry M. Toschi, OSJ, 25–58. Guardian of the Redeemer Books, 2002.

Valabek, Redemptus M., O.Carm. *Mary, Mother of Carmel: Our Lady and the Saints of Carmel*, Vol. 1. Edizioni Carmelitane, 2001.

Wilson, Christopher C. "'Living Among Jesus, Mary, and Joseph': Images of St Teresa of Ávila with the Holy Family in Spanish Colonial Art." In *The Holy Family in Art and Devotion*, edited by Joseph F. Chorpenning, OSFS, 24–36. Saint Joseph's University Press, 1998.

Wilson, Christopher C. "Saint Teresa of Ávila's Martyrdom: Images of Her Transverberation in Mexican Colonial Painting." *Anales del Instituto de Investigaciones Estéticas* 74–75 (1999): 211–33.

Xiberta, Bartolomé Mª., O.Carm. "Flores josefinas en la liturgia carmelitana antigua." *Estudios Josefinos* 17 (1963): 301–19.

About the Authors

Joseph F. Chorpenning, OSFS, is President of the International Commission for Salesian Studies (ICSS) and chairs the International Salesian Research Seminar. He received his PhD in Romance Languages from The Johns Hopkins University and STL in Historical Theology from The Catholic University of America. He did postdoctoral studies in Art History at New York University's Institute of Fine Arts. He is a priest of the Wilmington-Philadelphia Province of the Oblates of Saint Francis de Sales. For twenty-seven years, he served as Editorial Director of Saint Joseph's University Press in Philadelphia (1997–2024). He is the author of numerous publications in Carmelite Studies and on Saint Joseph and the Holy Family. He also organized pioneering exhibitions of Latin American Viceregal art focused on Saint Joseph (1992) and the Holy Family (1996) at Saint Joseph's University. He has been interviewed about his research on Saint Joseph by national media outlets, including Catholic News Agency, Fox News, and Time magazine. He is a charter member of The International Josephology Society (TIJS), for which he serves as Program Officer.

Steven Payne, OCD, is the endowed Chair of Carmelite Studies and ordinary professor of theology at The Catholic University of America. He received a doctorate in philosophy from Cornell University in 1982 and a doctorate in theology from The Catholic University of America in 2000. He is a priest of the Washington Province of Discalced Carmelites. He is current president of the Carmelite Institute of North America, former principal of Tangaza University College (Nairobi), former editor of *Spiritual Life* magazine and ICS Publications, and the author of *The Carmelite Tradition* (Liturgical Press, 2011), as well as numerous other works on Carmelite topics.

Index

Ambrose, Saint
   Commentary on Luke, 16
Anne of Jesus, Blessed, 8n4
Anne of Saint Bartholomew, Blessed, 8n4
Annual Lecture in Carmelite Studies, 3, 7, 58
Apocryphal Gospel of Pseudo-Matthew, 63
Aquilina, Mike, 58
Augustine, Saint, 18

Basilica of the Sacred Heart (Rome), 48, 49
Bavaro, Raffaele Maria
   Istoria di San Giuseppe, 70
Beas, 40, 41
Benedict XIV, Pope, 63
Bernard of Clairvaux, Saint, 50
Bernardine of Siena, Saint, 31
Bostius, Arnold, 64
Brussels, 12

Cannistrà, Saverio, 74
Carmelite(s)
   General Superiors, 3, 11
   Marian orientation, 63

Carmelites of the Ancient Observance
   eremitical charism, 34, 36
   liturgical veneration of Saint Joseph, 9, 12, 16–18, 23–24, 46, 52, 64–66, 69
   Province of the Most Pure Heart of Mary, 2
Casanate, Girolamo, Cardinal, 69
Catholic University of America, The, 2, 4, 5, 7
Center for Carmelite Studies, 2, 4, 5
Chorpenning, Joseph F., 3, 4, 59
Clouwet, Peeter, 13
commonplace, 9
COVID-19, 74

d'Ailly, Pierre, 18, 21
   The Twelve Honors of Saint Joseph, 16, 17, 24
Dictionnaire de spiritualité, 8
Diepenbeeck, Abraham van
   The Hermits of Mount Carmel Visited by the Holy Family, 13, 14
Doze, André, 28

Earthly Trinity, 13, 15, 16
Elijah (the prophet), 45, 63, 67, 68
Elisha (the prophet), 45, 68

Francis, Pope, 9, 48, 57
  Homily of March 19, 2020, 62, 72
  Patris Corde, 9, 52, 59
Franciscans, 63
French Revolution, 51

Gerson, Jean, 11, 13, 16, 63
Giovanni di Gesù Maria
  Instruction for Novices, 68
Gracián, Jerónimo, 29, 40, 67
  Josephina: Summary of the Excellencies of Saint Joseph, 8n4, 45
Gutiérrez, Joaquín
  Saint Joseph Protecting the Teresian Carmel, 21, 22, 40–41

Happel, Stephen, 7
Holy Family of Jesus, Mary, and Joseph, 28, 33–34, 35, 37, 38, 63, 66
Huizinga, Johan
  Autumntide of the Middle Ages, 18n24

Immaculate Conception, 47–48
Industrial Revolution, 51
Ite ad Ioseph, 50, 52

Jesus Christ, 16, 21, 28, 29, 31, 33–34, 37, 41, 48, 50, 52, 53, 58, 64, 65, 66, 74

Salvator Mundi, 50
Joachim and Anne, 63
John of the Cross, 68
John Paul II, Pope Saint, 8, 48, 57
  Redemptoris Custos, 8, 53, 57
Joseph of Egypt, 50–51
Joseph, Saint, 1, 3
  adoption by Teresa of Ávila as her father, 28, 55
  Carmelite veneration of, 11–12, 16–18, 23–24, 63–69
  cloak, 40–41, 43, 44
  contemplative, 37–38n50
  Eucharistic dimension, 64
  faber (artisan), 16
  father of Jesus on earth, 16–18, 48, 58, 59, 64–65
  Feast (before 1969) / Solemnity (since 1969) (March 19), 53, 55, 57, 61, 71, 72
  Feast (1955–1969) / Memorial (since 1969) of Saint Joseph the Worker (May 1), 55, 56, 57, 71, 72
  Feast of the Patronage (1680–1911) / Solemnity of Saint Joseph (1911–1955), 46, 52, 53, 54, 55, 69, 70, 71, 72
  founder of Teresian Carmel, 38, 67
  heavenly physician, 1, 25, 27
  husband of Mary, 18, 48, 53, 57, 59, 65, 71
  intercessor in every need, 1, 24, 31–33
  model of Carmelite life, 29–31, 37, 65

opifex (worker), 55
patron / protector of Carmel, 2, 45, 66–74
Patron of the Universal Church, 3, 9, 46, 47, 48, 49, 50, 52, 55, 57, 58, 62, 71
pre-Tridentine Carmelite proper office and Mass, 12, 16–18, 64–66
protector of Teresa of Ávila during perilous journeys, 40, 41
role of Teresa of Ávila in promoting veneration of, 5, 7–9, 29–33, 38–39, 66–68
spouse of the Virgin Mary, 18, 64–66
teacher of prayer, 3–4, 29–31
universal mandate, 68
Juan de la Concepción, 69
Juan de San José, 69

Laredo, Bernardino de
Ascent of Mount Sion, 31
Leo XIII, Pope, 48
Quamquam Pluries, 8, 74
Lombard, Peter, 18n24

Mary Magdalene de' Pazzi, 65
Mary, the mother of Jesus, 10, 11, 12, 16, 17–18, 21, 24, 28–30, 33–34, 37, 40, 45, 48, 50, 52, 53, 57, 59, 62–67, 71, 74
Mater Dolorosa, 50
Memory aid (*machina memorialis*), 10
Mercurian, Everard, 38n50

Mérode Altarpiece (also known as the *Mérode Triptych* and *Annunciation Triptych*), 18–21
Monastery of the Incarnation (Ávila), 23, 24, 25, 34–35
Monastery of Saint Joseph (Ávila), 1–2, 37–38
Montreal, 8
Morresco, Daryl, 5
mousetrap(s), 18, 21

O'Neill, Míċeál, 74

Paul VI, Pope Saint, 57
Payne, Steven, 5
Pius IX, Pope, 3, 9, 46, 48
Inclytus Patriarcha Joseph, 70
Quemadmodum Deus, 50, 71
Pius X, Pope Saint, 53
Pius XII, Pope, 55
Power, David N., 7
puritas cordis (purity of heart), 65

Revised Liturgical Calendar (1969), 57
Ribera, Francisco de, 38n50
Rollini, Giuseppe
Saint Joseph, Patron of the Universal Church, 48–52

Sardi, Giuseppe Maria, 70
Sullivan, John, 7

Teresa of Ávila
Book of Her Life, 1, 26
Book of the Foundations, 36
development of apostolic and ecclesial dimension of eremitical charism, 36

Teresa of Ávila *(continued)*
  predilection for visual images, 10
  promoter of devotion to Saint Joseph, 5, 7–9, 29–33, 38–39, 66–68
  qualities of her relationship with Saint Joseph, 26
  transverberation, 34, 35
  Way of Perfection, 36
triptych, 10
  virtual triptych, 10, 13
Tritemio, Giovanni, 63

Valladolid, 8
Vatican Council I, 71
Vatican Council II, 53, 71
Viteleschi, Muzio, 38n50

Whitefriars Hall
  Carmelitana Collection, 7, 27

Year of Saint Joseph, 3, 9n6, 58

Also in Studies in the Carmelite Tradition

What Makes a Carmelite a Carmelite?
Exploring Carmel's Charism
by Keith J. Egan
Introduction by Steven Payne, OCD

The Personalism of Edith Stein
A Synthesis of Thomism and Phenomenology
by Robert McNamara

Also from The Catholic University of America Press

Being Unfolded
Edith Stein on the Meaning of Being
by Thomas Gricoski
Foreword by William Desmond

Thine Own Self
Individuality in Edith Stein's Later Writings
by Sarah Borden Sharkey

The English Critical Edition of the Collected Works of Karol Wojtyła / John Paul II
Volume 1
Person and Act and Related Essays
Volume 2
The Lublin Lectures and Works on Max Scheler

Available from cuapress.org

ICS PUBLICATIONS
Edith Stein: The Complete Works: Critical English Edition
Volume 12
Finite and Eternal Being
An Attempt to Ascend to the Meaning of Being
by Edith Stein
Translated by Walter Redmond

MOTHER TERESA INSTITUTE
Mother Teresa: Just a Pencil in God's Hand
Reflections in Honor of a Saint
Edited by Brian Kolodiejchuk, MC

Mother Teresa's General Letters to Her Sisters
Edited by Brian Kolodiejchuk, MC

Review for Religious is a Catholic journal that promotes the study of Catholic religious life and its relationship to God, the Church, and the world. The journal features peer-reviewed articles and reviews of books. Published twice annually, contributions from a wide variety of fields, disciplines, and perspectives are welcome.

Review for Religious is published by the Conference of Major Superiors of Men with The Catholic University of America Press. Subscribe at https://www.reviewforreligious.com/discover/

Center for Carmelite Studies
School of Theology and Religious Studies
Catholic University of America
620 Michigan Avenue, NE
Washington, DC 20064

(202) 319-6045
trs-carmelite-studies@cua.edu

The mission of the Center for Carmelite Studies is to make the resources of this rich Carmelite heritage available to the contemporary church and world, by fostering scholarly study and research in the history, culture, and spirituality of the Carmelites, and promoting the effective pastoral application of the results.

Carmelite Center Activities
- Developing graduate courses and programs on major figures, movements, and themes in the Carmelite tradition.
- Identifying additional lecturers and scholars who can collaborate in the delivery of these courses and programs.
- Offering scholarship support and dissertation guidance for doctoral students wishing to focus on a Carmelite topic.
- Organizing and/or co-sponsoring conferences, symposia, workshops, and lecture series related to the Carmelite tradition.
- Promoting scholarly publications and the development of bibliographical resources in the area of Carmelite Studies.
- Developing practical training and orientation programs for lay colleagues in Carmelite ministries and others who could benefit from deeper exposure to the Carmelite heritage.
- Collaborating with other scholars and scholarly organizations involved in Carmelite Studies, and sharing information about their activities and resources.

www.ingramcontent.com/pod-product-compliance
Lightning Source LLC
Chambersburg PA
CBHW051457290426
44109CB00016B/1787